Solving Religion with Logic

*Logical proof that God exists
and the Bible is all true*

Paul Kasch

ISBN-13: 978-1482616309

ISBN-10: 1482616300

Table of Contents

Preface

Does a spiritual dimension exist beyond the physical one we can see, feel, hear, and touch?

If so, which of the world's religions, if any, is truth?

It is the goal of this book to definitively reach a concrete answer to both questions, starting from an entirely neutral position, using nothing more than the widely available human intellect. The finished product of this work would not exist if the quest failed. Since you are reading this, the answers are indeed available, and, as you will see, can be proven with logic. That is exactly what the following pages will do. Before arriving at the conclusions, we must first clear our minds of all preconceived biases, devise an efficient work process, and then work our way through the naturally occurring issues which present themselves in the solving of such a serious dilemma.

The act of posing these two questions is by itself something of great debate. Many would insist they are not the proper questions to ask, and still others will not concede the logic of the second question following the first. This can only be the result of existing biases, because the assumption of a positive answer to the first question innately gives birth to the second.

The first question is asked because it encompasses the implications of the world's most popular religious teachings, and the purpose of this work is to resolve, in finality, the many conflicting beliefs. Should we determine that a spiritual dimension does in fact exist, it follows that the next natural query is that of further details; its nature, its relationship with the physical dimension, and in what manner it may be accessed. If this information is knowable, it is reasonable to suppose that some person (or group of persons) who has dedicated themselves towards research on the subject may have already uncovered useful data on it. The search for answers should, therefore, naturally start with what has already been presented. Perhaps we can save ourselves the unnecessary work of reinventing the wheel. After analyzing all of the available information and proving or disproving it with unwavering, sound logic tests, we may or may not need to continue digging on our own for the much sought-after truth.

A fair objection, before we begin, is: Does it matter? If a spiritual dimension does exist, and if (at least some) knowledge of it is attainable by those of us living in the physical dimension, is it a worthwhile pursuit? Will coming into this knowledge have any potential benefits for a person, either in this life or in a possible continued existence beyond it? Several of the world's largest religions insist that it not only matters, but it matters so greatly, that all other concerns are trivial by comparison.

However, there are some opposing religious and philosophical viewpoints which state that nothing matters at all. In other words, nothing a person thinks, feels, or believes has any bearing whatsoever on their mortal or immortal fates. The diversity of existing beliefs among the world's religions is so great that it is unlikely a person could invent anything new if they tried. Whatever you can reasonably come up with on your own and decide to believe in, there is probably a group of people out there already vehemently teaching it as truth.

It is not the purpose of this book to accommodate self-derived religious truths. It is to determine whether or not there is a sovereign religious truth, through the use of a rational thought process. Inventiveness has no place in a quest to discover the self-evident.

While we must start from an entirely neutral position, we do know in advance that conflicting viewpoints cannot both be truth. This is only obvious, and needs no further logical dissection. Therefore, before we even begin, we can conclude that religious philosophies which attempt to embrace multiple opposing beliefs are pure nonsense, and as such, are wholly underserving of any consideration whatsoever. An example of this is *Unitarian Universalism*. If I say a plum is the one true God and you say the plum is only a piece of fruit but your bicycle is the one true God, perhaps one of us is right – but a third party who insists we are both correct can only be dismissed as a useless babbler who is wasting everyone's time.

Opposing teachings cannot both be true, any more than east and west can both be the same direction.

When it comes to answering the question of importance, one must logically conclude that the findings of our search could possibly be the most critical thing one ever considers. This is due to its unquantifiable potential. Our mortal lifespan is a finite, observable, measurable phenomenon. The prospect of an eternal existence dwarfs the mortal lifespan to such an unfathomable degree, it is rendered insignificant by comparison. To suggest this irrelevant speck of mortality controls the destiny of the immeasurable eternity is to speak of leverage so powerful it is beyond comprehension – but that is precisely our concern.

"Aha!" you say (and rightly so), where did I come up with this concept of eternity if we are supposed to be starting our investigation from a void and neutral mindset? By using a justifiable bit of foresight. If the conclusion to our first question proves to be yes, then the second question, which is unavoidable at that point, will force us to first research what is already claimed to be found. We can see this potential development well in advance, so it is not unreasonable to consider the possible consequences now. It is merely a matter of looking before we leap, which is generally considered wise. Since I live on planet earth surrounded by people and culture, I already know quite a bit about the beliefs of the world's largest religions. Most of them teach, to one degree or another, that what we do here during our short tenure in the physical dimension determines our welfare in the eternity beyond. To put it another way, should the spiritual dimension prove to be there, the next thing we will be doing is examining those kinds of claims, searching for a logically provable truth.

Therefore, we are unavoidably cognizant of the potential importance of our investigation before we begin. It is so potentially important, in fact, that perhaps no other activity can soundly be justified until we find the answer, or at least determine with a great degree of certainty that the answer is not discoverable. The weightiness of the matter has often been described in a metaphor known as *Pascal's Wager*, the logic of which is difficult to dispute. It's basically a risk vs. reward decision. A famous preacher once paraphrased Pascal's Wager by saying:

*If heaven doesn't exist, nothing matters. If heaven does exist, nothing **else** matters.*

Opponents of Pascal's wager argue that in order to comply with the wisdom of it, one must know which religion "to bet on," and having to make a choice between so many opposing beliefs exposes the futility of the notion. Why should one assume Biblical Christianity, the religious viewpoint most often referred to with Pascal's Wager, to be the obvious take-it-or-leave-it proposition for placing one's hope in an eternal paradise? These objectors do bring up a valid-seeming point, at least from their perspective. We will seek to solve their dilemma (assuming they actually care, which is a big assumption) when and if we arrive at our second question. Indeed; if we cannot resolve the second question, the findings of the first question are not beneficial, even if we conclude beyond every last doubt that the answer is yes.

Those who have read my other books know I am a Bible-believing Christian. My detractors will no doubt insist that as such, an unbiased, neutral starting point is impossible for me to achieve. Perhaps they are right in a personal sense, but such a complete brainwashing is unnecessary being as logical conclusions will stand or fall on their own merit, regardless of the personal biases of the one presenting them. Assuming a neutral position (the best we can), and then seeing if we can honestly work our way out of it using only facts and reason is all that is needed here. If the logic is unsound, the conclusions will fail miserably and categorically. Don't go anywhere. You are going to have a very difficult time finding any weak links in our developments and conclusions.

Let's face facts: we are all biased in our beliefs. This cannot be helped, because we are the product of our life's experiences. If you were brought up in a Seventh-day Adventist church, for example, I will have a hard time convincing you God approves of my diet and church attendance schedule regardless of how skilled a debater I happen to be. Deeply ingrained beliefs do not exit at the first sign of a logical argument.

Yet, we need to subject ourselves to logic and sound reasoning in order to make important decisions in this life. It's all we have going for us. If we really were created by a deity, then it is the deity who supplied us with our intellect, so it is a safe conclusion that our creator intended for us to use it. It even stands to reason that honestly exercising our deity-provided intellect may lead us to the truth about our creator. (There happens to be a Bible verse which promises we will find God when we truly open our hearts and search for Him, but I digress.)

We must first clear our hearts and open our minds if we are to genuinely seek unbiased religious truth. Yes, assuming a position of spiritual neutrality may be difficult to do for some, but it can be accomplished – enough for our purposes anyway – with effort and a little mental exercise. That is what we will strive for in the next chapter.

Solving Religion with Logic

Assuming the Semi-Agnostic Viewpoint

If we are going to use reason to arrive at religious truth, we must begin from a position of impartiality. The first order of business is to determine the proper starting position, which must be an attitude free of any religious biases or philosophical leanings. Of all the possible existing religious viewpoints, the one which is most suited for our purpose is agnosticism, with a slight modification. This is the viewpoint we need to assume.

Why not start from the atheist viewpoint, some may ask. Atheism is an extreme position, one which is doctrinally unyielding. Atheists believe something very specific with much conviction. This attitude is unbending. It cannot suffice for our purposes, because it is heavily biased, far from impartial.

Atheists dogmatically believe there is no spiritual dimension, based on a lack of immediately discernible evidence. Our purpose is to discover whether or not an unseen dimension exists, but atheism dismisses such a notion in advance purely on the basis that it is unseen. Holding the firm opinion that the term 'invisible quarry' is an oxymoron does not properly equip a person who is on a quest for an invisible quarry. Their preconceived notion will likely keep them from acknowledging the quarry even should it present itself in a straightforward manner.

It is interesting that atheists claim to have already solved the very dilemma we are concerned about. Are we wasting our time with this entire project, then? Hardly. Atheism is just another conflicting religious view in the world, and an extreme one at that. As such, it deserves no more special preference than any of the others if we fervently desire to discover truth. This is an investigation, so we are concerned with facts and logic, not hardened opinions. If the atheists turn out to be right, logic will force us to arrive at their conclusion all on our own, soon enough.

Many people misunderstand atheism. Logically speaking, the absence of a sound supporting argument renders the position *there is no God* no more valid than the position that your friend's bicycle is God. Atheists seem to have successfully distributed a widely held misnomer throughout modern popular culture; that their position is the naturally logical one, and consequently the onus of proof lies with everyone else. This reasoning fails miserably, and it's important to understand why, in order to assume the proper semi-agnostic viewpoint we need to conduct our investigation. Their conclusions are based on assumptions; largely the assumption that the unseen does not exist merely because it is unseen. It is an unsound argument.

If you have ever argued with an atheist, you probably know better than to try that again. Usually, their (rather weak) arguments about unseen = unreal are expected to be conceded as obvious truth, and those refusing to acknowledge such a glaring transparency are thought to be either lacking in intelligence or emotionally unstable, or both. Religious people who wisely avoid arguments with atheists are typically tolerated by them in social gatherings, but are categorized as emotionally insecure unfortunates whose intellect is apparently insufficient to save them from feeling a need to believe in something silly. That kind of superiority complex appears to be a by-product of atheism, but it is sorrowfully unfounded, and so logically flawed that it leaves one wondering just who the poor shmuck born with the inferior intellect really is. One only needs to look around a little before becoming forced to acknowledge the presence of intelligent individuals holding radically opposing religious viewpoints. Some of these individuals have IQ's north of 170 and would be considered by professional psychologists as perfectly healthy specimens. The very existence of such people shatters the foundation of the atheist allusion that their position is drawn from "common sense."

The reason for presenting such a detailed defusing of one particular religious viewpoint here is because it is probably the biggest obstacle in obtaining a neutral stance, at least in the western culture where this book will be available. Moreover, atheism is often mistakenly thought of as an impartial attitude, when nothing could actually be further from the truth. Most atheists are no more interested in a search for truth than a radical Islamic terrorist is; both seek to defend their existing, familiar, comfortable beliefs at all costs, and will continue to do so even if faced with overwhelming logical evidence to the contrary. That attitude cannot help us in our task.

The agnostic viewpoint is much more subjective, except for one annoying facet of it which we need to weed out before we can adopt it. Agnosticism, on the surface, simply shrugs and says, "I don't know." Agnostics do not arrogantly suppose they possess extraordinary knowledge of the universe (or of possible multi-dimensional plains of existence). They do not dismiss the idea that an invisible realm may exist on the grounds that they cannot see it or have not personally experienced it. They say, "I don't know, maybe."

The problem with true agnosticism is it goes one inexplicable step further and states matter-of-factly that the knowledge cannot be attained. This conclusion is so unsound, and so contrary to the core doctrinal attitudes of agnosticism, that it renders the entire belief system a contradiction of itself, erasing it from the logical map entirely. How do you preach 'not knowing' in one breath, then turn around and assert you 'know' the knowledge cannot be attained in the next? It is an irreconcilable conflict in terms.

In so considering, we see that the viewpoint is really just a cop-out. Someone who adheres to agnosticism in a strict sense holds the attitude that the discovery of religious truth cannot be reliably accomplished in this life. They concede that any one of the world's popular religious teachings may be correct, or none of them – they cannot tell, so they wash their hands of the entire matter. A person making such a claim appears to be rather easily dissuaded and not particularly interested in discovering truth. Therefore, the position of agnosticism can rightfully be labeled an excuse for laziness. We have already touched upon the potential importance of our investigation. To not make the attempt because the task seems daunting is akin to not stepping off the railroad tracks as a train approaches because one is not sure if it will stop before it reaches them.

Still, it is possible that our investigation will prove to be inconclusive. In that case, however, we will concede only that *we* were not able to arrive at the answers. We will refrain from arrogantly purporting that it cannot be done purely on the basis of our own efforts having come up short. Perhaps our efforts will suffer from misdirection, or not be carried out diligently. Perhaps we will find we are unqualified, as a bus driver may be if asked to write an article explaining quantum physics. One person (or group of persons) who fails at an attempt to accomplish something does not logically conclude that the task is impossible – especially if the person trying gives up rather easily and never really has their heart in it. If that were the case, Mount Everest would never have been climbed and the four-minute mile would never have been broken.

Moving forward then, we must take on a semi-agnostic position to begin our work. Specifically, we will assume an attitude that *we don't know*, and everything must be proven. This includes the notion of whether or not the knowledge can be attained. No doctrinal assumptions will be held as we begin to examine our environment seeking an apparent, logically-provable religious truth. Having first pointed out the logical flaws in strict agnosticism and the heavily-biased nature of atheism, it is hoped that we can now clearly see our way to a neutral mindset.

Atheism, however, remains a logically-viable candidate for our conclusion. It would seem that all we have to do is prove God doesn't exist, and as difficult as that may sound at first, we remain open to it because: we don't know.

True agnosticism, on the other hand, can never be our final conclusion because the belief system logically contradicts itself. We don't know if the knowledge can be attained. If it turns out that it can, we will attain it and agnosticism will be disproven. If we fall short, we cannot logically conclude that the knowledge is unattainable just because we failed, so we will remain in a position of not knowing if it can be attained. Should all else fail, the position we end up in will be the same one we start from, which answers all the following questions more or less accordingly:

Is there a God? We don't know.

Can we find out if there is a God? We don't know.

Is the Bible a hoax? We don't know.

Is it possible to verify the things written in the Bible? We don't know.

Is there life after death? We don't know.

Do humans have a spirit? We don't know.

Was Muhammad a prophet? We don't know.

Was Joseph Smith a prophet? We don't know.

Are the writings of Mary Baker Eddy just a bunch of silly nonsense? We don't know.

Are there many roads to God? We don't know.

Are there multiple Gods? We don't know.

Are we all little mini-gods who will someday be in charge of our own planet if we live right? We don't know.

Did the Jesus of the Bible actually live and exist? Yes, this is historical fact.

Was Jesus a good guy and a good teacher who lived 2,000 years ago, but ultimately just a man? No, this is not logically possible, so we cannot even start with "we don't know" on this one. Jesus claimed to be the Son of God; therefore, he was either a liar, a lunatic, or what he claimed to be. He must be one of those three. Which ...we don't know. Liars by definition are not good people, and lunatics are not good teachers, so the answer to this question must be no.

Was Jesus an angelic creature, like Michael the archangel in the Bible? This is possible if angelic creatures are subject to lunacy or lying and misrepresenting themselves, so we don't know. But we can at least logically conclude he was not an honest angel, because he claimed to be the Son of God; therefore, he is either a liar (angel or not), a lunatic, or what he claimed to be. He must be one of those three. Which, we don't know.

Is the devil real? We don't know.

Is there an innate, universally definable difference between good and evil somehow, or is it all up to individual values? We don't know.

Are ghosts and haunted houses real? We don't know.

Did dinosaurs really live on the earth? The logical evidence must conclude yes. Exactly when, we don't know. Carbon dating techniques are relatively new and have not been proven accurate.

How old is the earth? We don't know. Radiogenic dating techniques are still largely a theory and have not been proven accurate. Therefore, there is no reliable dating technique available, and even if there were, it is possible the earth was created in an aged state, much in the same way the Bible describes Adam having been created as a full-grown man and not an infant.

Did man evolve from ape-like creatures? We don't know.

Is vertical evolution a valid theory? We don't know.

Can the Bible and evolution both be true? There are some working theories on this, so let's just say we don't know (for now, anyway).

Is there an eternal hell? We don't know.

Is it possible that the Bible is true, yet the existence of hell is not? No, because the Bible says there is an eternal hell. At least parts of the Bible must be untrue for the eternal hell not to exist. We don't know which of these may be true, if either.

Can an honest religion embrace different faiths? No, because the teachings of different faiths directly conflict with each other. All attendees would need to be converted to new doctrines for agreement to take place, in which case the individual members would no longer be a believer in the teachings of their original faith. Most likely, a church or religion which claims to embrace multiple faiths is in reality practicing a subtle method of proselytizing.

Was the Bible divinely inspired? We don't know.

17

Did God conceal religious truth from man for thousands of years and then finally decide to reveal it through one person, just a few hundred years ago? We don't know.

Was Jesus the promised Messiah of Israel? We don't know.

Did Israel exist as a nation (or nations) in the Palestine area in ancient times? Yes, this is a historical fact.

Is it possible for some people to talk to the dead? We don't know.

Are the accounts of near-death experiences real? We don't know.

Is religion the opiate of the masses? We don't know.

Are atheists smarter than religious people, on average? No, and this is a verifiable fact. They are not less intelligent on average, either. Atheism is simply another religious viewpoint and there are people who score high on intelligence tests belonging to every religion on the planet.

If heaven exists, what do you have to do to get in? We don't know.

How can finite man have fellowship with an infinite God? We don't know.

Is man inherently bad or inherently good? Define bad and good please. In any case, we don't know.

Did the universe start as an explosion in space a long time ago? We don't know.

Is all life on earth just the result of cosmic happenstance? We don't know.

Is there any purpose to life? See the previous question please, as the answer is dependent upon the answer to that one.

Are you getting the idea here? We are opening our minds to all possibilities in regards to religious truth, but closing our minds to all violations of logic and denials of known facts. This is the only rational way to begin a search for truth.

A question might now be asked as to whether religious truth can be found outside of the realm of logic. After all, faith is often defined as belief in things not seen. We must reject this notion whole-heartedly, because it leaves us no recourse. Also, we find no breach of reason in allowing for the possibility of the unseen to exist. That is, in fact, our very quest – to see if the existence of the unseen can be proven using logic.

If truth can exist outside of logic, then what we exist in must be complete chaos. Looking around at the world we live in, we see order, not chaos. Patterns of reliable consequences are easily observable in our physical dimension. This refutes the suggestion that we exist in complete chaos, therefore any universal truth must be verifiable within the confines of rational deduction. Without logic, nothing can be proven, and criminals cannot be convicted. Similarly, an illogical religious claim is as unappealing as it is useless. With so many conflicting religious beliefs surrounding us, logic is our only hope of resolving them. Many will cling to their irrational beliefs come what may; we must leave them to their own musings.

You and I, however, possess sound reasoning ability, and are about to put it to good use. We have opened our minds to all that does not breach valid logical deduction. We are properly equipped for getting to the bottom of "this whole religion thing," if there is one to be gotten to.

Before we begin, we should first examine our motives for conducting the investigation in the first place, and come to the conclusion that they are logically founded. If we cannot do that, the idea of verifying religious truth becomes an empty pursuit. In that case, we may as well forget the entire project and just stay in our semi-agnostic mindset.

Validating the Investigation Motives

Now that we have assumed an open-minded and unbiased position, we should ask ourselves a few questions. Is it a logical pursuit to investigate religious truth? Can we reasonably defend the motives for wanting to take on this task? Or are we succumbing to a purely emotional desire? Would Mr. Spock approve of this project?

In order to honestly define our motives, we should first remove emotion from our thought process. This is not easy to do, and, in fact, may be an illogical effort. Emotions are part of the human makeup and cannot be completely separated from our rationale. This is why colleges offer classes in logic; so we can train ourselves to recognize sound and unsound arguments. The training will kick in and hold us to reason when our emotions would sidetrack us into possible unsound conclusions. It is highly advisable to study the basics of logic (perhaps by reading a short book on the subject) before making important decisions in life that are based upon analyzing conflicting claims.

A sound argument comes to a logical conclusion only by drawing further inferences from a beginning statement which is assumed to be true. You need to have a foundation of agreed upon truth to use as a starting point. The professor in your logic class will not open for debate the merit of the starting statements used in the example arguments. The students are instructed to accept them as truth, and all further statements are weighed against that assumption. For example, a starting statement may well be something like: *all space aliens have five eyes*.

In our case, however, we must have a universally agreed upon starting statement in order to proceed. At the moment, we want to know if the pursuit of religious truth is a logical project to undertake. I now ask the reader to agree with me on the following:

• We are humans living on planet earth.

• We must eat, breathe, drink, and sleep in order to remain alive.

• Most humans prefer to sleep inside a structure of some sort, indoors, and refer to this structure as *home*.

• Humans are congregated into groups on planet earth, definable by race, nationality, and country.

• Sometimes, individual humans become angry or upset; other times, they do not.

• Groups of humans from individual countries have fought wars with groups of humans from other countries all throughout recorded history.

This is enough to get us started. We must agree on all of the above or there is no point in going further. I have lived on this planet for nearly fifty years now, have been educated and socialized in a manner consistent with most of my readers, and have had many conversations with other people in my lifetime. Because of that, I can make a fairly safe assumption that a person who does not agree with all of the above points is not accepting statements that are generally thought to be obvious, verifiable facts by the overwhelming majority of educated people on our planet. It is, therefore, a reasonable starting point for a sound argument.

Now, in order to eat and maintain a home, we must work to some degree or another. Even those of us who are wealthy must at least lift food to our mouth and chew it, which requires effort. It is possible to have others do all the work for you, but somebody, you or another person, must work in order for you to be able to eat and keep a place to sleep indoors.

In order to accomplish the work which maintains our lives, some level of education is necessary. A person must learn how to perform the work which provides them with nourishment and shelter. Seeking knowledge is not only logical, but necessary.

Seeking knowledge does not stop at bare minimum necessity for most people. I draw this conclusion by simply observing the environment I exist in. Countries have fought wars with each other all throughout recorded human history; in order to do so, knowledge of how to conduct warfare had to be sought. I see schools, colleges, and institutions of higher learning in most major cities of western civilization. Many states and countries have laws which force children to attend school until a certain age, and at these schools a much higher degree of knowledge is imparted than what is required for providing basic human necessities. The latest statistics in the USA show that well more than half of high school graduates typically enroll in college seeking an even higher education.

Because I exist in a society, I am quite aware that many humans hold religious beliefs. I cannot drive very far before seeing a church of one type or another along the roadside. I also know, at least to a small degree, the basic elements of some of these belief systems. This cannot be helped. There is a television and radio in my house. There are newspapers and magazines in public places. Conversations with other people reveal bits and pieces of information about some of these religious beliefs. The names of the Christian God are commonly used as swear words by many people, and the number of the year we use on our calendars is counted from a major religious event which supposedly happened a little more than 2,000 years ago. None of this information could be avoided; I gained it simply by living and functioning as a normal member of the culture I found myself living in.

Many of the larger religions believe in some form of life after death, that one's consciousness continues to exist in an unseen spiritual dimension. Some religions assert that this continued spiritual existence will last for an eternity and be extremely pleasant or extremely unpleasant, depending upon decisions I make while I am alive here in the physical dimension. I did not need to go seeking this information; at a very early age, I saw cartoon cats die and become angels playing harps on clouds or descend into fiery caverns.

The death rate for humans living on planet earth is 100%. This conclusion is drawn from the fact that the oldest documented human alive today is less than 120 years old, and the oldest documented human life span recorded in modern times is less than 130 years. Logically, I can assume with certainty that I will die someday.

I also know, through no special efforts on my part, that some religions claim there is a benevolent, all-powerful God who created us and loves us, much in the same manner as human parents love their own children.

I do not believe any of the above mentioned knowledge can be avoided by a person living in western society. Whether deliberately seeking it would have been a logical pursuit or not, I cannot tell, and do not wish to speculate upon. I can only acknowledge that the information is already there in my mind as the result of normal, functional living in the world I was born into. It couldn't be helped. My only choice is whether to investigate some of it or ignore it all.

Knowing what every other person living my culture knows about religion, and not having deliberately sought this information, I now need to establish a personal opinion about it. If I decide I am not interested, that is a valid decision, but a decision nonetheless and an opinion has been established, that of disinterest. If I decide to do some research before first forming an opinion, that is an alternative decision, one which is not lacking in sound reason any more than deciding upon disinterest. If I decide to form a firm opinion without performing any kind of research or investigation first, that is also a valid decision, but one which is directed by emotion rather than factual research.

If an all-powerful God exists who created me and loves me, it logically follows that this entity would be interested in my welfare and perhaps be willing to direct some of that power to my benefit. It is not unreasonable to ponder over the possibility of God's power assisting me in my work and daily tasks. It is, therefore, entirely logical to investigate whether this particular religious viewpoint has any validity, as doing so would fall within the category of seeking knowledge for the provision of basic necessities.

Sometimes, individual humans become angry or upset. We cannot deny the fact that emotions are a significant part of the human makeup. While we can deliberately apply sound reasoning to arrive at answers to questions, we can never be completely emotionless. One of the primary driving human emotions is the desire for love; to love and be loved. It

26

has been scientifically observed that individual humans who feel they are loved tend to become angry and upset less often, and less severely, than those who do not feel this way. Therefore, it is a logical pursuit to investigate claims which state it is possible to enter into a beneficial relationship with an all-powerful God who loves me the way a parent loves a child. Notice this decision is logically arrived at, not emotionally, even though the purpose of the decision is to satisfy an emotional need.

It would be irrational for me to immediately dismiss the concept of the possible existence of an unseen spiritual dimension purely on the basis that it cannot be seen, being as *unseen* is part of its very definition. I must have other reasons for this dismissal to be logical, some kind of compelling evidence to the contrary. It is, however, a defendable position from a logic standpoint to be disinterested.

The religious claims that decisions made in this finite lifetime determine whether a continuing consciousness in an infinite spiritual dimension will be spent pleasantly or unpleasantly may be offensive and even outrageous-seeming on the surface. Those are emotional reactions, however. The implications of such claims are monumental. We cannot pretend the claims do not exist, because they have permeated our culture to such a large degree they are unavoidable. We saw the cartoon cats going to heaven or hell when we were three years old. Such a widespread teaching with such unfathomable potential consequences cannot be rationally dismissed without doing a little due diligence first. The stakes are too high and the teachings are too popular to prudently ignore.

In conclusion, we have determined with much clarity that the quest for religious truth is an entirely logical pursuit. In fact, in view of what we have just discussed, a sound argument can be made that neglecting such a task would be reckless.

Solving Existence

We have come to understand that seeking religious truth is a rational, wise pursuit. We have obtained an impartial viewpoint for conducting our research. Where to start, then? It is probably best to begin in the same manner we began to examine our motives. That is, start with a universally agreed upon truth which is easily observable by simply waking up in the morning, opening our eyes, and looking about ourselves.

I cannot logically deny that I exist. I have eyes that see and ears which hear, so I must acknowledge the environment I exist in as well. This is a big, round, blue planet I live on. It is surrounded by a vast, immeasurable universe consisting of an uncountable number of stars and other planets. It's all there. It exists.

What's it doing there? How did it all get there? Where did life on planet earth come from, and what are we humans doing here? These are natural, logical questions to ask as we take note of our obvious existence and observe our environment.

Many people take the existence of the physical dimension we live in for granted. A person disinterested in science, religion, and philosophy has no choice but to do so. By taking it for granted, one is assuming its existence is natural and unremarkable. Is this a logical stance?

On one hand, the physical dimension is there, and we are here in the middle of it, and there doesn't seem to be much we can do about it. We wake up and we are hungry and want to get something to eat. That's all we really need to think about, but it is a purely reactionary agenda, as a baby bird who is much more concerned about mom coming back with breakfast than about marveling over the nest and surrounding tree. Humans are not animals living a purely reaction-based life. We read, study, and think about things. All those institutions of higher learning that 68% of high school graduates enroll in offer many classes which specialize in the contemplation of our environment and the properties of our physical dimension.

In order to fully grasp the concept of existence, it helps to try to imagine non-existence for a moment. Not your personal existence, but the existence of everything; the entire universe. Not the *contents* of the universe, but the very universe which houses its contents. (In truth, the universe itself is merely a content of the physical dimension.)

Imagine the instantaneous removal of all matter, all planets, all stars, and everything you can see or touch, from the universe. What do we have left? Some gasses floating around in space maybe? Remove those, too. Now what's left? Elementary particles perhaps;

molecules, atoms, and quarks – remove all of those now, too. Everything is gone. What's left? Just empty space, right? Many people suppose the empty space that now remains is "nothing," which is incorrect. That empty space is still *something*. The physical dimension remains, even after we have removed everything from our universe. In order to truly have nothing, that empty space needs to be removed as well. Are you able to grasp this? Many people cannot, and these are the folks who take for granted the presence of the physical dimension. Deeper thinkers, however, can at least partially glimpse the concept of true nothingness, the removal of the physical dimension itself. Such a notion probably cannot fully be comprehended by the human mind, but many are able to at least understand the idea here. If you are one of them, you will then better comprehend the philosophical question of existence. Why is the physical dimension here? Why should anything at all exist, even completely empty space?

When considered in this context, the possible existence of a spiritual dimension is not such a distant thought. It is no more illogical than the existence of a physical dimension when pondering the idea of existence. The implications can be staggering to consider. Perhaps intelligent life forms in a spiritual dimension debate whether or not a physical realm actually exists.

Back to the question of how the physical universe we see around us got there. One possible explanation is that some intelligent force intentionally created it.

31

This logically opens the reverse possibility; that it was not intentionally created. Therefore, all possible detailed explanations must fall under one of these basic precepts. Either the universe was intentionally created, or it wasn't. If it was, the next line of logical pursuit is to the nature and origin of the creators, and whether or not they still exist and can be found. This is the fundamental purpose of seeking religious truth.

If the universe was not intentionally created, then it must have happened as the result of random chance. In this case, we ourselves, and everything around us, are the product of cosmic accident. Many insist that this is the obvious answer, but just as many see it as an impossibly far-fetched notion. The detractors of the cosmic accident theory will point to mathematical equations which result in outrageously large numbers in calculating the odds against the series of accidents which would have to happen for even the first living organism to come into existence by random chance (or to put it scientifically, by *spontaneous generation*). Proponents of the cosmic accident theory state that it doesn't matter what the odds were, obviously it happened, because we are here, and our existence as we know it is just one possible outcome in an infinite number of cosmic accident chain reaction events, with each outcome just as unlikely as any other, but one of them had to happen, and here we are.

It is this debate which we now must logically solve. If the cosmic accident theory holds up under the scrutiny of valid reasoning, our mission is over. We can then confidently conclude there is no religious truth, and existence is all an accident. If the cosmic accident theory fails to hold up, we then can conclude there must be a religious truth, religious truth being defined as the nature, origin, and whereabouts of the force which created the universe and discovering whether or not we may come into some type of beneficial relationship with such an entity (or entities). This is because the failure of the cosmic accident theory to hold up only leaves the alternative of intentional design. There are no other possibilities. Either the universe was intentionally designed or it was not; if it was not, then it had to be a cosmic accident because a lack of design necessarily concludes accident.

The Large and the Small of It

Scientists have observed that stars and galaxies in the universe are moving away from each other, in all directions, in the same manner that matter outwardly moves away from other matter during an explosion. This is why we are said to be living in an *expanding universe*. Planets are held in place by the force of gravity around their respective stars, but the solar systems themselves are moving in an outward expanding motion away from each other. If the stars are moving away from each other, they must have been closer together at one time. This obvious conclusion has been carried even further into a theory that all matter in the universe was at one time condensed into a very small and very dense point no bigger than a pea. Something caused it to explode, and that is where the physical seen universe originated from, an explosion in space a long time ago. Everything you see out there in the night sky, the unfathomable and unknown totality of it all, was once all condensed into a very small ball you could hold in your hand – at least, that's how the *big bang* theory goes.

There is no explanation as to what caused the explosion, however, or how that small dense ball of matter came into being in the first place. There is also no logical reason to carry the expansion of the universe back so far as to originally be the size of a pea, or, for that matter, to stop at the size of a pea. Why not even smaller, as the size of a speck of pepper, or the size of an atom, or even the size of a *quark* or *neutrino*, or even smaller particles which have yet to be observed by human instruments, such as those that make up quarks or neutrinos. If you can keep imagining things smaller and smaller, you will exhaust your mind's ability to grasp it at some point. Whatever the very smallest observable physical particle is, it is extremely likely to be made up of even smaller particles which have yet to be observed, and whatever those are may be made up of even smaller particles, and so on and so on for who knows how far, perhaps infinity. It's an absolutely mind-blowing possibility, upsetting as it may be. There is no rational reason to stop at the size of a pea in determining the original size of the universe in the big bang theory. The only safe assumption is that stars used to be closer to each other; how much closer is a matter of speculation, and what caused them to start moving away from each other only theory.

Grasping the infinitely large is just as futile an effort as attempting to grasp the infinitely small. The size of the entire universe has been speculated upon by some scientists, a size much larger than the observable universe – but if there is a limit to its size, what lies beyond is a real problem for the human mind. However, even grasping the size of the observable universe is not so easy. The general consensus among astronomers, using the latest human instruments, is 46 billion light years in scope. That means to travel from one side of it to the other, at the speed of light, it would take 46 billion years (by which time it will have expanded and have become even larger, so the actual trip would take significantly longer).

Somehow, astronomers have speculated the size of the entire universe is currently around 156 billion light years wide. This is in conjunction with an estimated age of the universe being 14 billion years old, since the explosion which started it all.

Even if we are able to grasp the scope of something 156 billion light years in size, it is impossible to grasp the scope of what may lie beyond it. What's out there – infinite empty space? Other universes? If there are other universes, aren't they part of the physical dimension as well? If the physical dimension is limited in size, and stops at some point, what is beyond it? Nothingness? How far into the nothingness can you go? Is there just a wall, stopping you from going further? How thick is the wall? What does it feel like when you run into it – is it hard like concrete or spongy and cushiony? What exactly is beyond the wall? What are the properties of nothingness?

There is a fantastic interactive zooming scale of the universe at the website **htwins.net,** in which you can zoom down to the incredibly minute and zoom out to the incredibly large. At the very largest viewpoint, the estimated size of the universe is enclosed by a border. This is convenient for the web page, but in reality of course, something must be there at the outer edge, perhaps continuation into empty space or a barrier of some sort. If it is a barrier of some sort, it must have a measurable thickness and something must exist beyond it. At the extreme opposite end of the scale, the small end, several levels beyond the neutrino, you see the elements of *string theory* and *quantum foam*, which are only theories. In fact, you get into the theory area before you even reach the quark section on this scale, being as quarks and neutrinos are not observable with human instruments, and their existence is only assumed by observing the behavior of space around them. If the strings and the foam at the smallest level do actually exist, they too must be made up of even smaller parts – right? The scale obviously stops at the limits of human knowledge and current physics theories. If it did not; and instead accurately continued to reveal all that there is, it could logically continue in both directions forever. There is no rational stopping point on either side, only an emotional desire for one from our brains.

Many quantum physicists will disagree and insist that there must be some limit, some elementary particle which has no further substructure and simply exists. This is not a logical assumption, however, being as all observable particles of matter have always been found to be made up of smaller parts, down to the very limits of our observation abilities. There is a fascinating discussion on this topic at the website **QuantumDiaries.org**; search for: *But what are quarks made of?* ...and give it a read if you are interested in this topic. Because solid objects exist, they must be made of particles which contain mass, so any substructure must also be made of particles which contain mass, ad infinitum. What the elementary particle theories are attempting to do is stop the logical continuation of zooming in for infinity, and fulfill an emotional need to find some limitations to our physical environment. This strikes me as vain, as it assumes a great degree of significance to our particular level on the universal scale. A hypothetical ability to continue zooming in on an "elementary particle" with an ever-powerful zoom lens should eventually reveal *some* substructure, don't you think? At which point the process could continue, forever.

This apparent infinite scale of our physical existence is disturbing. The human mind cries out for mercy at some point, and demands a stopping point on both ends. We'll call the estimated size of the known universe the upper size limit, and just put a wall around it and say that's it, and refuse to speculate on the thickness of that wall, what it is made out of, or the physical properties of the nothingness beyond it. We will call the theoretical neutrino the smallest particle and insist it is not made from any smaller parts; that it is all just one yellow round thing, all the same element, and an infinitely powerful microscope will only show it is all the same substance with no smaller parts or structure. This we do for human comfort, not from logical reasoning. The truth we wish to ignore is that there are no logical limits in scaling out for a bigger picture view, or zooming in for a closer one. It is extremely possible, perhaps even likely, that our entire universe is a neutrino in somebody else's universe, and conversely, that our neutrino houses somebody else's entire universe, and that this structure continues in both directions ad infinitum.

The reality before our eyes is that we apparently live right smack in the middle of downtown eternity, as it infinitely extends in both directions the way the universal scale only begins to show us. This notion cannot be logically denied, only emotionally. There is no reasonable stopping point in either direction, other than the limits of what we humans can observe with our highest-tech instruments. On the large side, I can always ask *what is beyond that* and there must always be an answer, even if it is the further continuation of infinitely empty space. On the small side, I can always ask what the smallest level is made of, so we can always zoom in further. Should an infinitely zooming microscope exist, it could always take us smaller, as long as there is something which contains physical properties for us to focus in on, and there must always be – otherwise no physical object could exist at all. Everything we have been able to zoom in on has always had a structure, made up from smaller parts, so there is no reason to suppose an end to that pattern, or speculate on where it may be, other than desperate human emotions crying out for one. Such a stopping point cannot even be rationally conceived. Those who state they cannot accept the concept of eternity need only look up at the sky at night or peer into a microscope to see that it lies before their very eyes, right here in the physical dimension.

It is interesting that the pattern of smaller-mass objects orbiting larger ones is consistent at all levels on the scale. Inside an atom, electrons orbit the nucleus (which is a cluster of protons and neutrons) in the same manner planets orbit stars. Entire galaxies rotate around their own central points, where there are thought to be great black holes consisting of unfathomable gravitational mass. If we were able to zoom out of our entire universe, and keep going until it appeared as a small dot, I would expect to see other universes appearing as small dots, all of them rotating around a central great mass in the same manner that electrons rotate around a nucleus. If we were able to zoom down inside of an electron, I would expect to find a substructure which fits the same pattern. The Andromeda galaxy is only a tiny speck of light in the sky to our naked eye, and an atom is also only a tiny dot in the microscope until the magnification on the lens is increased.

Some scientific theories of how our universe originated do not subscribe to the idea of a small ball of matter exploding, but rather to some floating gasses in empty space exploding, resulting in the creation of matter. These theories do not explain where the explosive gasses came from, however. Considering the scale issues we just discussed, speculation on the nature of the big bang becomes a bit of a moot point. On which portion of the scale did the originating explosion begin? If each neutrino may house an entire universe, as is entirely possible, the big bang could have originated a billion neutrinos down on the scale somewhere.

Then there is time, which is sometimes referred to as the fourth dimension. Time has been theorized to be inconsistent and run independently in different locations, depending upon its relationship with cosmic elements. That idea in turn leads to the notion that time is actually physically intertwined with observable objects. This is known as the *space-time continuum* theory, and has been largely adopted by physicists because it allows their other theories about the universe to work together more smoothly. It has been speculated by physicists that other universes may indeed exist outside of our own, and in their own time, which may or may not overlap with the time element in our own universe.

As you can see, the facts and theories about the physical universe around us are unsatisfying. Ultimately, they result in more questions than answers, and there is no cosmic accident theory which attempts to solve the existence of the physical dimension itself. If an explosion in space a long time ago explains the formation of our universe, fine – but that only explains the formation of something which is housed within the physical dimension, so it does not really even address the question of existence.

Origin and Development of Life

Is there at least a satisfying explanation as to the origination of life forms on planet earth? If our planet was just the happenstance result of a cosmic explosion, where did the first life form come from? How did we get life from non-life?

In the 1950's, two scientists by the names of Dr. Stanley Miller and Dr. Sidney Fox conducted laboratory experiments which successfully converted inorganic materials into organic materials. Specifically, amino acids were formed by rearranging molecules through chemicals and electricity in laboratory tests meant to mimic conditions of an early, lifeless earth. Amino acids are a biologically important compound found in all living organisms, and are particularly necessary in the makeup of proteins.

It is thereby theorized that this is how life began on earth; first by amino acid molecules naturally occurring through chemical reactions with lightning or volcanic activity, then the amino acids accidentally forming into various more complex molecules, some of them being proteins. Through a chain reaction of chance occurrences, the proteins then formed into living cells, the living cells then, by chance, arranged themselves into simple living creatures such as sea worms. Chance occurrence after chance occurrence then caused the sea worms to molecularly rearrange themselves into a variety of more complex creatures, and the chance occurrences just kept coming until one day some of those accidentally rearranged molecules were hitting golf balls on the moon. Disregarding the improbability of it all for moment, what we should first be concerned with is if this scenario playing out is possible at all. After all, proponents of this theory do have a valid point in that some result or another must occur after a gazillion chance occurrences of chemicals and particles interacting with each other, and each result is equally unlikely as any other.

But – this result? Can it possibly have happened by accident?

For chemicals and energy to combine in a way that would result in the spontaneous generation of a living cell, the amino acids would first need form the required proteins. That would just be the beginning of a long, detailed, complicated process. Proteins are considered the basic building blocks of all life. Even the simplest life forms require a specific variety of them, arranged in a specific manner. Famous chemist Dr. Wilder-Smith, an English physicist holding professorships at many universities in numerous countries, calculated the odds of even the simplest, smallest protein cell forming by chance occurrence to be more than 10 to the 67th power to one against. This would be assuming an ideal atmosphere with an abundant supply of ideal chemicals provided, given an allowable time of 100 billion years (10 to 20 times longer than the latest estimates of the earth's age) where that ideal atmosphere is sustained the entire time. The number 10 to the 67th power means a 1 with 67 zeroes after it. Mathematicians generally agree that any number greater than 10 to the 50th power has zero chance of ever occurring.

Dr. Wilder-Smith concluded: *"It is emphatically the case that life could NOT arise spontaneously in a primeval soup of this kind."*

Dr. James Coppege, a recognized scientist and published author, built upon Dr. Wilder-Smith's research and came to a similar conclusion: *"The probability of a single protein molecule being arranged by chance is, 1 in 10-161 power, using all the atoms on earth and allowing all the time since the world began...for a minimum set of required 239 protein molecules for the smallest theoretical life, the probability is, 1 in 10-119,879 power. It would take, 10-119,879 power, years on average to get a set of such proteins. That is 10-119,831 times the assumed age of the earth and is a figure with 119,831 zeros."*

Imbedded within each cell of every living organism is a nucleus containing chromosomes. Zoom in on the chromosomes and you will see the DNA structure for that particular organism. DNA is extremely complex. Every living thing has its own unique DNA arrangement, even bacteria. There are millions of components to even the simplest DNA structure. The mixing of chemicals does not produce DNA. Only DNA creates more DNA. It is possible for DNA to change structurally upon the reproduction of itself, but there is no other way for DNA to form other than to be reproduced from existing DNA. So, DNA had to exist in order for more DNA to come into existence. Where did it originally come from? There are some theories that the originating DNA on earth came from outer space, but that does not answer the ensuing question of where the DNA from space came from.

Researcher and mathematician I.L. Cohen had this to say about DNA and evolution:

"At that moment, when the DNA/RNA system became understood, the debate between Evolutionists and Creationists should have come to a screeching halt. ...the implications of the DNA/RNA were obvious and clear. Mathematically speaking, based on probability concepts, there is no possibility that Evolution was the mechanism that created the

approximately 6,000,000 species of plants and animals we recognize today."

Even taking for granted the pre-existence of an original DNA structure, renown mathematician and astronomer Sir Fred Hoyle calculated the odds of a living cell forming by natural process, given an estimated age of the earth of 4.6 billion years, to be about 1 in 10 to the 40,000th power. That is a figure with forty thousand zeros. Remember, a figure with more than 50 zeros is agreed by mathematicians to have zero chance of occurring.

There are some animals on the earth which would seem to defy the concept of vertical evolution. One of them is the lowly (and quite stupid) sheep. It is a known fact sheep cannot survive without human care. They must be sheared, or they will die. How did such an animal evolve on its' own? Another such animal is the bombardier beetle. This strange bug shoots a fiery explosion out of its butt as a self-defense mechanism. The flammable chemicals are housed in separate compartments and shot out into the air behind it, where they mix and explode. How could this creature have evolved without blowing itself up?

When examined, the spontaneous generation of life theory has such serious challenges one must wonder as to why Darwin's theory of evolution is still taught in schools. The following two quotes from Nobel Prize winning Harvard University evolutionary scientists will provide the answer:

"There are only two possibilities as to how life arose; one is spontaneous generation arising to evolution, the other is a supernatural creative act of God, there is no third possibility. Spontaneous generation that life arose from non-living matter was scientifically disproved 120 years ago by Louis Pasteur and others. That leaves us with only one possible conclusion; that life arose as a creative act of God. I will not accept that philosophically because I do not want to believe in God, therefore I choose to believe in that which I know is scientifically impossible, spontaneous generation arising to evolution."

--**Dr. George Wald**, evolutionist, Professor Emeritus of Biology at the University at Harvard, Nobel Prize winner in Biology.

"We take the side of science in spite of the patent absurdity of some of its constructs, in spite of its failure to fulfill many of its extravagant promises of health and life, in spite of the tolerance of the scientific community for unsubstantiated just-so stories, because we have a prior commitment, a commitment to materialism.

It is not that the methods and institutions of science somehow compel us to accept a material explanation of the phenomenal world, but, on the contrary, that we are forced by our a priori adherence to material causes to create an apparatus of investigation and a set of concepts that produce material explanations, no matter how counter-intuitive, no matter how mystifying to the uninitiated. Moreover, that

46

materialism is an absolute, for we cannot allow a Divine Foot in the door."

--**Professor Richard Lewontin**, geneticist, Professor of Biology at Harvard University.

Both of the above men are highly esteemed professors of evolutionary science at one of the world's most legendary institutions of higher learning. What they state is an acknowledgment of what we have discovered for ourselves in this section; that the idea of spontaneous generation of life on earth, followed by evolution of species, is scientifically impossible and they know it. They still *choose* to believe in it, however, even though they acknowledge it is not possible, because there is only one alternative – and they are *philosophically* opposed to the alternative.

The quotes in this section only scratch the surface of similar statements made by qualified experts in the field of evolution. A quick internet search for 'evolutionist quotes' will lead you to hundreds of them. Taking the time to read through the web pages found in the first several pages of search results will reveal that all such statements made by educated, respected researchers seem to be arriving at the same conclusion; that there is not a shred of evidence supporting evolution, and there is much evidence refuting it. Now, you can certainly find opposing opinions by individuals with high IQ's and who hold respectable positions in the scientific community – but, as Gerald Wald admitted above, those opinions are philosophically grounded, not scientifically, and, in fact, take their stance in glaring opposition to undeniable scientific data. The fact that even some credible scientists admit what they believe in is impossible serves to destroy the strength of the theory (and we cannot find a higher authority on the matter than a Nobel prize-winning Harvard professor of evolutionary biology), because if evolution were true, there would be universally agreed-upon supporting scientific evidence of it

Conclusion

Search as we may, there is no satisfactory explanation for the existence of our physical dimension. All theories of where we came from and how we got here (outside of creation) take for granted the preexistence of the physical dimension which houses our universe. Theories of how our universe started do not even address the question of existence. The same can be said of the DNA structure for living organisms; DNA cannot have come from anything but other DNA, so some kind of DNA must have always existed. This simply won't do as an acceptable answer.

Eternity appears to exist right before our very eyes, as there is no rational way to hypothesize a stopping point on smaller and smaller particles of matter, nor a limit to the continuous zooming out views of the larger and larger.

Our environment is delicate, which makes our existence all the more amazing. Theories about the earth which place its age in the billions of years would make the continued existence of life on earth even more confounding; that a delicate environment would accidentally hold together and support life for such a long time. If we exist by cosmic accident, it is extremely likely a cosmic accident would end that existence before now, with all these random chance encounters of chemicals and energy happening all the time, all around us. Famous physicist Stephen Hawking addressed this phenomenon when he stated:

"The universe and the Laws of Physics seem to have been specifically designed for us. If any one of about 40 physical qualities had more than slightly different values, life as we know it could not exist: Either atoms would not be stable, or they wouldn't combine into molecules, or the stars wouldn't form heavier elements, or the universe would collapse before life could develop, and so on..."

--**Stephen Hawking**, considered the best known scientist since Albert Einstein, Austin American-Statesmen, October 19, 1997

Many qualified experts in the field of evolutionary science admit the science is a fraud and the theories have proven to be impossible. While some experts do hold opposing opinions, the fact that the theory is debatable among the experts at all reveals a lack of evidence supporting the theory. If life started by spontaneous generation followed by evolution of species, the evidence would be there for all to see and it would be undeniable. Instead, leading experts in the field of evolution state just the opposite, that what is undeniable is the theory has proven to be false. Some of these experts further state they still choose to believe in what they know is impossible rather than to acknowledge the only remaining alternative, which implies a religious truth.

Finally, we cannot deny mathematical equations. When we begin to disagree that 2+2 = 4, we leave the realm of rational thought. That simple math equation has infinite inferences, some of which we have built upon to create the fields of higher mathematics. Those higher fields reveal the impossibility of life on earth having begun by spontaneous generation. Therefore, to cling to the belief of spontaneous generation of life is to mathematically assert that 2+2 does not equal 4. This is the real nail in the coffin.

We cannot logically exist by the result of a cosmic accident, and the existence of the cosmos in which such an accident may have occurred cannot be explained. If we are not the product of accident, the only alternative is that we are the product of design. We have no choice but to logically conclude we were intentionally created. Ergo, there must be a religious truth.

Solving Religion

Astounding as it may seem, we have solved the question of our existence. Perhaps even more amazing, we were able to accomplish this using nothing more than a rational thought process to analyze what we can see all around us, and what we know from scientific facts about the living organisms on our planet. The conclusion is logically unavoidable: Life on earth was not an accident, so it must have been intentionally created. This we now know. Hence, it has become desirable, perhaps even urgent, to solve the question of religion as well.

Our definition of religious truth is accurate information about the force (or forces) which created life on earth; any and all factual data we can gather regarding that force, especially whether or not a person can enter into a beneficial relationship with it.

So, what do we know right out the gate? Well, the force that created us is either still paying attention to us, or it isn't. One of those two conditions must be true. If it is no longer paying attention to us, then it is impossible for us to enter into a beneficial relationship with it; in this case, the discovery of a religious truth will be of no special consequence. It is, therefore, logical to assign investigations into this particular scenario a lower priority than investigations into possible answers which do have potentially important consequences.

We also know the force must be intelligent, at least by human standards. Since we have proven the cosmic accident theory to be wrong, we know there was intention behind our creation. The designs of the protein and DNA cells are extremely complex. The delicate balance of nature in our environment was obviously intelligently designed. Whatever created us knew more about our science than we do.

Either our creators desired for us to have the religious truth, or they did not. If they did not, it is logical to assume such a truth may be unattainable, given that whatever created us possesses such a higher degree of intelligence and ability than we do. If our creators did desire for us to find the truth, then it logically follows that the truth may very likely already have been discovered, being as humans have populated this earth for many thousands of years now. If the creative force desired for us to have the truth but we do not have it, this would indicate the creative force failed in this respect, which seems unlikely given all that it did accomplish, and the high level of intelligence and ability the creative force apparently possesses. Therefore, it is appropriate to begin the investigation by looking at existing religious beliefs, logically dissecting them in search for a provable truth.

By disproving the cosmic accident theory, we have already eliminated atheism as a potential religious truth, as the cosmic accident theory is a central doctrinal belief for atheists (since they have no alternative but to acknowledge creation). True agnosticism has also been logically eliminated because it is a contradiction of itself, proclaiming *no knowledge* but at the same time insisting it has knowledge that there is no knowledge. Admitting defeat in our own search for religious truth is still on the table, however, and will be our default position should no other truth be provable. We know we were created, but by whom or what we do not yet know, nor do we know whether or not we can actually attain that information.

We also have already eliminated obvious contradictions of logic; religious viewpoints which attempt to accept that two opposing religious beliefs can both be true (examples include the Bahá'í Faith, Scientology, the Unification Church, and Unitarian Universalism). We cannot even entertain such a notion without abandoning sound reason.

Similarly, we can immediately dismiss religious teachings which state that "it doesn't matter" what a person believes, because that would reduce our investigation to an exercise in futility. If the truth is not beneficial to us, then there is not much point in pursuing it, so we will assign research into non-beneficial truths a low priority. Should such a viewpoint hold the actual religious truth, we will get close to it eventually upon failure to complete our task, and it will remain one of the possible (and likely improvable) truths which are encompassed by the implications of our failure. Therefore, we don't need to waste any energy on this type of thing.

The remaining religious viewpoints fall into two broad categories: *monotheism*, the belief that the creator is a single deity who is one God, and *polytheism*, the belief in multiple deities which may or may not include a creator deity. There are many subcategories under each of these, but all must ultimately boil down to a belief in one God or multiple gods. We can immediately dismiss polytheistic religions which do not include a creator deity, since we have already proven we were created, and such a religious viewpoint does not even attempt to provide us with our definition of religious truth. Likewise, any philosophically-based religion which does not attempt to provide knowledge of creation or a creator need not even be considered (for example, most forms of Buddhism and Humanism). Thankfully, this greatly reduces our potential candidates.

To recap: If a discoverable religious truth exists, our vastly superior creator(s) must not have intentionally hidden it from us; therefore, it has likely already been discovered. We:

1) ...are not interested (yet) in investigating religious beliefs which have no potential benefits if discovered to be true, and

2) ...have eliminated all religious beliefs which offer no explanation of creation or knowledge of our

creator(s) because they do not fit our definition of religious truth.

That leaves us an interesting list of potentials to begin our research with, including some polytheistic religions that offer an explanation of creation and claim benefits for their believers.

Assembling the Primary Candidates

Monotheistic Candidates

• Pantheism (includes some forms of Hinduism)

• Panentheism (includes some forms of Hinduism)

• Judaism

• Christianity (all denominations)

• Islam (all varieties)

• Modern "revelations" which modify the Bible

• Gnosticism

• Spiritism

• Zoroastrianism

• Some Buddhism modifications which include creation stories

<u>Polytheistic Candidates</u>

• Some forms of Hinduism

• Shintoism

• Ahl-e Haqq

• Some Buddhism modifications which include creation stories

• Paganism (includes all other forms of polytheism)

There is our primary list of potential candidates. It includes every major religious belief that does not logically contradict itself, allow opposing beliefs, neglect to provide information about our creator(s), or has already been disproven when we disproved the cosmic accident theory. If you don't see one you are looking for on the above list, and it has not already been eliminated in one of the methods just mentioned, it probably can be sub-categorized under one of the above. If not, perhaps it is a very small religion with relatively few followers, and we will search those out if/when we can eliminate all of the above.

Further definitions and categorization explanations are now needed for our candidates, as some are broad categories themselves which contain diverse beliefs and conflicting doctrinal teachings within them.

Pantheism: Religious belief systems which fall into this category do not believe in a separate spiritual dimension, but rather that it is contained within the physical dimension through thought and feeling. Consequently, the physical dimension we can see and feel is all there is. Pantheists believe all of existence is God, we are all parts of God, and everything that exists is part of God's makeup. God is not a separate being from creation. He is impersonal and unknowable. There is no conscious afterlife; upon death one's consciousness is absorbed into the whole of existence. The universe is explained as having created itself, as that is all there is. Many pantheists believe in reincarnation. Examples of Pantheistic religions include most forms of Hinduism (including Rajneeshism and Transcendental Meditation), Jainism, Taoism and Chinese folk religions, New Age beliefs, Theosophy, Rosicrucianism, and most forms of Buddhism.

Panentheism: Similar to pantheism but with the critical distinction that God has an additional, separate consciousness from the universe, although every component in the universe is still part of God. So, while all is still God, God also remains greater than the universe. This opens the door to explanations of creation, but these explanations of God creating the universe necessarily imply that he created it by *becoming* the universe, while still maintaining a separate consciousness from it. Panentheists do not believe in a conscious afterlife, only being absorbed into the whole of existence, with possible reincarnations of individual consciousness. Examples of panentheist religions include Sikhism, Tenriko, some forms of Hinduism, the Bahá'í Faith, some forms of Buddhism, and the New Thought movement (which encompasses Seicho-no-le, Religious Science, Jewish Science, and the Unity Church, among others).

Judaism: Believes the Old Testament of the Bible is God's inspired Word, but rejects Christ as the promised Messiah. Therefore, rejects the New Testament as inspired scripture. The Biblical accounts of creation and the afterlife are accepted from Old Testament scriptures. Not having the New Testament teachings, Judaism is foggier on the details of the afterlife than Christianity, not knowing whether the doctrine of *soul sleep* is Biblical or not. Judaism does believe in an eventual resurrection and afterlife, and also in the concept of hell.

Christianity: Accepts the New Testament writings as divinely inspired truth in addition to the Jewish Old Testament. Therefore, the entire Bible is considered truth – however, there is much dissention as to the interpretation of many scriptures within the many different Christian denominations and doctrinal teachings. The uniting cardinal doctrine is that Jesus is the Son of God and thus a divine being – not a creation – who became man and was willingly tortured to death as the only acceptable sacrifice for man's sin. The sacrifice of God's Son in this manner is referred to as the substitutionary atonement, as his death is considered payment for all sin. There is an eternal afterlife in a spiritual dimension (as well as possible additional physical dimensions). The afterlife will be spent in paradise or hell, depending upon one's rejection or acceptance of Christ as their Savior. Those seeking forgiveness of sins through his sacrifice are saved from hell. Examples of Christian denominations include Catholicism, Baptistism, Pentecostalism, Presbyterianism, Anglicanism, Lutheranism, Methodism, Seventh Day Adventism, and non-denominational belief in literal Bible truth, among others.

Islam: There are many varieties, but all are based on the teachings of Muhammad, a man who lived in the early 600's, some 230 years after the Bible was canonized. Muhammad's followers wrote the Quran, which is the written form of Muhammad's teachings. Islam teaches that the Bible contains some truth, but also some falsehoods wherever it conflicts with the Quran. The Quran was supposedly revealed to Muhammad by the angel Gabriel, a character from the Bible. These teachings include an eternal afterlife in a spiritual dimension which will be either in paradise or hell, depending upon God's decision, which will be based on whether your good works outweigh your bad works in this life. Specific doctrinal teachings within the various Islam sects vary widely, but all agree that Jesus was a prophet (and thus only a man) and his death, which was not by crucifixion, was not in any way atonement for man's sin. All Islam sects teach a works-based salvation. Islam agrees with the Bible in the case of the universe being God's creation.

Modern "revelations" which modify the Bible: We will define *modern* as having originated within the last 500 years, and *recent* as having originated within the last 200 years. There are many contemporary religious beliefs which fit under this category. These beliefs use the Bible as a starting point, but then claim further revelations, often through angelic visitation, which modify important points. All of these modifications change the Biblical view of who Jesus was, why he came, how he died, why he died, the sin nature of man, the existence of hell, and/or the urgent need for a savior. (Modifications other than those regarding Christ would place the belief under the umbrella of Christian denominations.) In particular, the atoning death of Christ on the cross as the sacrifice for man's sin is refuted in some manner or another in these beliefs, and usually results in a works-based salvation doctrine. Some claim that everyone is already saved, however. The Biblical notions of creation and the existence of a spiritual dimension are retained. Examples of religions in this category include Mormonism, Christian Science, Jehovah's Witnesses, Rastafarians, and Unitarianism, among others. In fact, Islam rightfully belongs in this category if we were only to remove the *modern* stipulation.

Gnosticism: A monotheistic belief which completely rejects the Bible and the teachings of most other religions. God created life through evolution and

60

human souls are reincarnated. God created other gods, deities beneath Himself, who also possess creation abilities. There are many varieties of Gnosticism beyond that basic premise, including some classical versions which believe the earth was created by an evil sub-god and all matter is evil. Gnostic salvation is very similar to pantheist/panentheist salvation in that once a satisfactory life has been lived, one is freed from the cycle of reincarnation and their consciousness is merged into the consciousness of many, which might make up the consciousness of God or one of the sub-gods, or, as some sects believe, a universal spiritual consciousness aside from God.

Spiritism: Commonly mistakenly referred to as *spiritualism* (even my word processor wants to change it to that), this religion advocates communication with the spirits of the dead, which are believed to be able to move back and forth between a spiritual dimension and the physical one. Practitioners of this religion believe God (the creator) condones this practice, and therefore must necessarily deny the Bible as a religious authority. The religion of spiritism believes in an eternal spiritual existence and an eternal progressive self-development after the death of the physical body.

Zoroastrianism: A declining Iranian religion, left over from ancient Persia, which is monotheistic and believes that God the creator is an enemy of chaos. There also exists a god of chaos, the enemy, a lesser god who will eventually be conquered. A spiritual dimension exists where departed souls reside until a day of resurrection when all will live in a physical dimension again for eternity. The purpose of existence is to fight against chaos and help bring an eventual end to it. While there are many similarities in this religion to God and Satan in the Bible, it is difficult to determine if they are believed to be the same entities.

Buddhism modifications: We listed this one under both monotheism and polytheism because some varieties assign a higher significance to a supreme being than others. All varieties believe in multiple deities. Buddhism in any form is similar to Gnosticism in many ways, but with highly regarded "Buddha" teachers, whom are considered deities in some variants, and even creators of the earth in others. The supreme being is an unknowable, impersonal energy force in all forms of Buddhism. The physical life is considered to be suffering, and human souls are continuously reincarnated until meditation techniques are mastered which allow one's soul to merge with a higher, universal spiritual consciousness.

Polytheistic Hinduism: Similar to Buddhism in essence, except that various deities are worshipped and appealed to for help, with no real thought toward the supreme being (who is really just an unknowable, impersonal energy force). Karma is a factor in determining when one may escape the cycle of reincarnation and merge with the higher universal consciousness; one must make up for bad karma in all past lives first.

Shintoism: A very old polytheistic Japanese religion which does not believe in a separate spiritual dimension. All of creation was spontaneously generated and gave birth to the first god. Humans are gods themselves. Upon death, a human continues to exist in spirit form. Some varieties of Shintoism assign the spirits a place among the living humans, others a special hell-like place located somewhere else in the physical dimension. What one does in their mortal life does not affect their continued spirit-life destination.

Ahl-e Haqq: A non-Islamic middle-eastern religion from the 14th century which is still popular in some parts of Iran and Iraq today, especially among the Kurds. They believe in both a physical and spiritual dimension, each realm having its own god. So, there are exactly two gods in this religion. Ahl-e Haqq is highly legalistic with a strict set of laws one must adhere to. Individuals are given exactly 1,001 lifetimes, through reincarnation, to live a perfect life that is successful in keeping all the laws. Upon completion of the perfect life, one's spirit enters an eternal paradise, where the spirit-realm god lives. Once you have blown it in the current lifetime, however, you can make some atonement to give you a little room for error in the next by adhering to the laws. If the 1,001 lifetimes expire without success, or if the *day of judgment* comes first (similar to the Biblical day of judgment), your soul is annihilated.

Paganism: A blanket term used to encompass all polytheistic beliefs; we will use it here as a catch-all for all other polytheistic religions. Examples would be Greek and Roman mythology, or modern voodoo.

What about Satanism and the occult? You may find this surprising, but these religious practices can best be categorized under Biblical beliefs or Bible modifications. Those who worship Satan or demons generally accept the Biblical revelation of these entities, and choose to align themselves with the devil rather than God. Some sects may distort the account of creation and assign portions of it to the demonic forces, and some may hope for an afterlife slightly better than the hottest parts of hell by "making friends with the devil," but generally speaking, these are Biblically-based belief systems. Any religious truth to be found here is more logically pursued in the Bible.

What about the many various ethnic/folk religions? These are small, not widely practiced (or even known), and difficult to quantify or even gain any information about. Most do not seek converts. Who knows what else is out there? A person can invent their own religion and have exactly two followers. Let's hope our search for truth doesn't come to this category, because it will be nearly impossible to investigate. We are forced to assign it a very low priority.

From the exercise of defining our primary candidates, we now find we are able to remove some of them based on logical conclusions in which we have already arrived. The first which jumps off the page at us is pantheism. By stating that the physical universe is God Himself, and there is nothing beyond, we are right back at the question of existence, which we have already solved. We know we were intentionally created, because it is the only alternative left after disproving the cosmic accident theory. Pantheism believes that the universe "created itself." This is illogical. All pantheism does is assign the existing universe the name of God. It does not actually believe in creation, or even address the issue. Therefore, it does not fit our definition of religious truth and the entire category can be removed. The theory appears to be a farce, really, semantics perhaps, and a play on words. Perhaps it is meant to be a thin veil over atheism, a place where atheists can be lovers of nature and not have to feel so arrogant.

Another problem with pantheism is there does not appear to be any appreciable benefits to it. Pantheistic Hinduism does claim to offer the "benefits" of learning how to commit permanent suicide from the physical dimension and put an end to one's individualism, the ultimate goal being to end the cycle of reincarnation (which nobody has any clear memories of anyway). Assuming one could even prove reincarnation, it is debatable as to whether ceasing to exist forever is preferable to having another life. In any case, we see no real urgency here, so even if we are to keep this possibility open, we can assign everything in this category a very low priority.

For that matter, all religious belief systems which include reincarnation and the ultimate goal of annihilation/absorption are highly questionable as to whether they offer any desirable benefits for the believer. The privilege of ceasing to exist only resonates with someone who truly believes that life is unbearable, and who expects their future reincarnations to be unbearable as well. The logic in such a notion is difficult to find. Most of us who live in western society acknowledge a degree of enjoyment in life. Even if we are deceived about that, and pantheism or panentheism holds religious truth somewhere, there certainly seems to be no hurry in arriving at it. After all, we appear to get ultimate second chances at achieving the goal, and it seems unlikely that those of us who find the concept foreign could make much progress at it in this life anyway. In the very least, we can assign all these religions a low priority (perhaps even lower than giving up on our investigation, as the implications seem so meaningless).

So, we can now remove **pantheism, pantheism**, all forms of **Hinduism**, all forms of **Buddhism**, and **Gnosticism**.

By contrast, **Ahl-e Haqq** threatens annihilation as your punishment for 1,001 failed reincarnations, while the above mentioned eastern religions dangle annihilation as their reward for eventual success. To the western mind, annihilation seems a more fitting punishment than a reward, so Ahl-e Haqq can stay on the table for now.

We can also remove **Shintoism** after looking at its definition a little closer. Creation giving birth to gods, as opposed to vice-versa, does not explain creation. The spontaneous generation of creation avoids the very question of creation; therefore, it does not really fit our definition of religious truth. Yes, an argument can be made that the gods in turn creating us does explain our own creation, so perhaps we should not be so hasty – however, the religion appears to have no useful benefits. Nothing a person does in this life affects their afterlife, so there is no pressing motivation to do anything. The practices of Shintoism amount to communicating with spirits in an effort to entertain them, and trying to be happy in life. It is more of an attitude than a religion. At best, this one is a low priority and can be removed from the list of primary candidates.

That whittles our list of actual candidates down to the following categories (some of which are still broad):

Monotheistic Candidates

• Judaism

• Christianity (all denominations)

• Islam (all varieties)

• Modern "revelations" which modify the Bible

• Spiritism

• Zoroastrianism

Polytheistic Candidates

• Ahl-e Haqq

• Paganism (includes all other forms of polytheism)

Wow – the list got short fast. Perhaps our work will not be so labor-intensive after all. Before we dive in, we should remind ourselves that we do not yet know if religious truth is to be found anywhere on the above list. Also, we do keep a lower-priority list of secondary candidates as a backup plan, should it come to that. The above list does seem to provide our best chances of success, however, as it includes all the logical candidates which could possibly reveal the desired information about our creator(s) and offer potential benefits. Let's move on to the elimination round.

Logically Seeking the Truth

A confusing predicament presents itself at this stage; that of the blatant conflict between these belief-systems. Each of them insists the others are wrong, and there are intelligent people who are fervently entrenched in each camp. If the truth can be found using only reason and logic, how is it that intelligent minds can hold dogmatically opposing beliefs? One begins to sympathize with the atheist viewpoint in this regard, and suspect human emotions of becoming stronger than human intellect. Our problem, of course, is that we have already proven creation, and now need to investigate religious claims seeking truth. Perhaps the discovery of that truth will provide some answers about the existence of such widely-held strong opposing beliefs.

In searching out the truth, it is desirable to work efficiently. We should choose a logical starting point with that in mind. By discovering a provable religious truth early on, we may potentially save ourselves from needless additional work. One religion proving to be truth would simultaneously prove opposing viewpoints false. We could then focus on doctrinal variants within the true religion, or perhaps investigate the phenomena of logically-flawed false religions which are able to seduce large numbers of intelligent minds.

If our creator(s) did not object to us discovering religious truth, it is reasonable to suspect that the truth may already have been found, given how long humans have lived on the earth. That is why we are starting with a list of primary candidates from the world's most popular religions – the ones which do not have logical contradictions, and which offer possible answers to our definition of religious truth. (Our definition of religious truth was naturally born from having proven creation; we now want further details and insights about it.) The candidates oppose one another for the most part, so they cannot all be true. We defined them after listing them, and were then able to remove many of them for logical contradictions, for failing to address our definition of religious truth, or for deprioritizing purposes due to a lack of perceived benefits. It is now time to prioritize the remaining candidates in the interest of work efficiency.

Two pertinent possibilities which exist are 1) religious truth has been known for a very long time, or 2) it has been discovered relatively recently. If our creator(s) did not object to us having the truth, it is reasonable to speculate that they may have actually desired for us to have it in the first place. In that case, given the obvious power and intelligence the creator(s) must possess, it follows that the truth would probably be known for a very long time by now. Even if the creator(s) are indifferent as to our discovering the truth, religion and higher thinking have been primary concerns of man from early times. If the truth is discoverable at all, it probably was discovered thousands of years ago. Modern technology is a great help in our scientific pursuits, but it has done very little to advance religion. If the truth has been known for a very long time and has survived the scrutiny of modern science, it figures to have a better chance of holding up under the scrutiny of logic as well. Therefore, in the interest of work efficiency, it makes sense to first analyze the oldest remaining religious beliefs on our list.

A decent argument can be made that paganism encompasses the oldest belief systems on the planet. This is probably true. However, they have not survived, at least in any appreciable numbers. An example would be the religion of the ancient Egyptians, which lasted some 3,000 years. It is a dead religion and not practiced today. Any religion which has not survived is less likely to hold truth than one that has, so dead religions can be deprioritized for now. Forms of paganism which are practiced today are relatively new. Now, there may be some remotely-practiced pagan religions in some places which have been handed down for many generations and qualify as being quite old. These are not logical candidates for us to start with due to their obscurity and lack of available information.

The most logical candidate to begin our analysis on will be very old and still widely practiced. The largest religion on planet earth at the time of this writing is Christianity. Because professing Christians generally believe the Bible is true, that also makes it one of the world's oldest religions. True, Christianity per se has only existed for a little more than 2,000 years, but Christians believe their religion is a continuation of Judaism and hold the Hebrew Scriptures as sacred. Certain books of the Old Testament are among the oldest written documents on earth.

The Bible is, therefore, the oldest religious text remaining on our list of candidates. Ancient Egyptian religious texts and ancient Hindu texts, which may predate the oldest books of the Bible, do exist, and some of the ancient Hindu texts are still in use – but neither of these are logical priorities, being as the Egyptian religion has not survived, and all forms of Hinduism are pantheistic/panentheistic, so have been rendered a low priority for a lack of perceived benefits and/or lack of creation explanation. Same goes for Taoism and Chinese folk religion, which are also very old.

The second largest religion is currently Islam, followed by atheism and agnosticism (no distinction is made between these for polling purposes), and then followed by a slew of our already deprioritized eastern pantheist/panentheist religions, finally followed by Spiritism and Judaism. The current list of the world's most popular religions, with our remaining primary candidates in bold, looks like this:

Christianity (all denoms): 2.1 billion followers

Islam (all sects): 1.5 billion followers

Agnostic/Atheist: 1.1 billion followers

Hinduism (all forms): 1 billion followers

Taoism / Chinese folk religions: 394 million followers

Buddhism (most forms): 376 million followers

Indigenous ethnic religions: 400 million followers

Sikhism: 23 million followers

Spiritism: 15 million followers

Judaism: 14 million followers

Baha'i: 7 million followers

Jainism: 4.2 million followers

Shinto: 4 million followers

Cao Dai (Modified Buddhism): 4 million followers

Zoroastrianism: 2.6 million followers

Tenrikyo: 2 million followers

Paganism: 1 million followers

Unitarian Universalism: 800 thousand followers

Scientology: 500 thousand followers

Christianity and Judaism are both Bible-based belief systems. Judaism claims the Old Testament of the Bible is truth, and Christianity is in agreement with Judaism on that point. These two candidates combined are by far the largest and oldest still-practiced religions left on our list. They are the logical starting point for work efficiency purposes. Perhaps we can kill two birds with one stone here. The best way to do that is probably to begin with the Old Testament of the Bible and treat that as a religion. If we can logically disprove the Old Testament, these two candidates can both be removed. If the Old Testament proves to be a religious truth, then it will be a simple matter of analyzing the New Testament to determine whether Christianity or Judaism is religious truth. At that point, we could then eliminate all blatantly conflicting beliefs, and proceed to examine all subsequent Bible-modifications to see if any are logically provable.

We need to define a process here, just so we are organized and know what we are looking for. We are setting out to prove a religious truth, not just agree that a story sounds pretty good. The religious truth must be an obvious, logical, inescapable conclusion arrived at in much the same manner as we were able to prove creation. These are the elements required to accomplish that:

1. The religious teachings must make **logical sense** and not include contradictions or conflicts.

2. The religious teachings must give us information about our creator(s) and **explain creation**.

3. The religious truth must be **available for anyone** who chooses to pursue it (otherwise its usefulness is questionable), and hopefully offer some appreciable potential **benefits** for the believer. If the truth is not open for everyone or there are no appreciable potential benefits, that does not disprove the religious belief – but it does render it a low priority, so it can be removed from the list of primary candidates before going any further.

4. The religious truth must somehow demonstrate its truth in such a convincing manner that it leaves no

74

logical alternative but to believe it. In other words, it must **prove itself** to be true, as we will not simply trust its teachings, any teachings, regardless of how logical they may *sound*. This is going to be the toughest part of the test. It may seem demanding of us, but as already mentioned, anyone can tell a good story. We need to see some irrefutable evidence beyond story. Hey, whatever created us is pretty darn powerful, right? This really isn't asking too much if you think about it.

We now have a logic-based four-point filter for examining religious claims. Anything passing on all four points must be true, because we demand that it prove itself on point four. Let's put our first candidate to the test.

Old Testament Analysis

The Old Testament of the Bible is also known as the Hebrew Bible, or the Hebrew Scriptures, or, in Hebrew, the *Tanakh*. It is divided into three sections: history/law, poetry/hymns, and prophecy.

The Old Testament consists of 39 "books" which were written by more than 25 different authors over a period of more than 1,000 years. The exact number of authors is not known due to some anonymous writings, and the exact date of some of the individual writings cannot be pinpointed. Scholars could get pretty close on the dates if it were not for the book of Job, which is of debatable origin among them. Many believe the book of Job is the oldest surviving written work on earth, having been passed on for many hundreds of years before being copied over again by Moses around 1500 BC. Others ascribe the original authorship to Moses.

The Hebrew canon of scriptures is said to be *divinely inspired*. Specifically, that the men who wrote the books were overcome by the *Spirit of God* when they wrote, which means the writings really came from God Himself. The writers are thought of as scribes who were only taking dictation from God.

The first five books of the Bible were written by Moses and are referred to in Judaism as *The Law*, although they also contain quite a bit of narrative history. The Old Testament begins with God creating the universe, the earth, and all life forms upon the earth, including the first man and woman – who soon commit the *original sin* in their disobedience to God. Creation and original sin is followed by the original populating of the earth. Man proves to be terribly sinful, and as a result God destroys all land-based life with a great flood except for one family He chose to save, that of Noah's. Noah's family begins the populating process over again after the floodwaters subside (including the repopulation of land-based animals from the ones God kept with them during the flood).

The following generations prove to be just as sinful, however. God then befriends one man, Abraham, and promises to make a great nation out of Abraham's descendants, who will be God's own people and represent Him on earth. Abraham's descendants grow into a large group, keeping to themselves while living in Egypt, where they are eventually made into slaves. God recruits a man named Moses to rescue them from Egypt, through a series of great and awesome miracles, and brings them into their own land which was promised to Abraham. The Jews prove to be a difficult people, however, and God has many problems with them. They do manage to come into the Promised Land and conquer it, with the help of God. That land becomes the nation of Israel, then and today. Moses dies before entering the Promised Land, but not before writing these first five books, which record the history of his people and give all the laws God instructed them to follow.

The next section of the Old Testament is a continuation of the history of the Jewish people in the newly-formed country of Israel. As they grow and populate, Israel has many wars with the surrounding Arab nations and experiences many periods of moral decay interspersed with religious rivals. God helps them at times and punishes them at other times. The biggest problem is their propensity to turn to idol worship and forget about God, especially during the good times. Through it all, God always has prophets, people whom He speaks to directly (often through visions and dreams), always trying to draw His people back to Him and back to following the laws of Moses.

After 400 years of being in the land, Israel has a civil war and splits into two Jewish nations, one in the north which retains the name of *Israel*, and one in the south known as *Judah*. Jerusalem is located in Judah, where the temple of God is, and where the people still have religious revivals and return to God frequently. The northern kingdom of Israel permanently turns to idol worship, however. God still performs many miracles through His prophets in both kingdoms all through their Old Testament histories. Eventually, God punishes both kingdoms by allowing them to be conquered and taken away captive. The northern kingdom is first to go in 721 BC to the Assyrians, followed by Judah to the Babylonians about 150 years later. Babylon was the first world empire.

God had foretold the punishment of His people should they turn away from Him, but also promised to keep a remnant of them, always, and eventually bring that remnant back into the Promised Land. The first occurrence of this was when the remnants of the Jews who were captive in Babylon were freed to return to their homeland by the Medo-Persian Empire. The Medes and Persians conquered Babylon seventy years into Judah's captivity there. The Jews returned and rebuilt Jerusalem, including the walls of the city and the great temple. This ends Old Testament history.

The next section of the Old Testament is poetry and hymns, all which are dedicated to the worship of God. This portion includes the book of Proverbs, which is supposed to be wisdom imparted directly from God to

78

King Solomon, the wisest man to ever live, according to the scriptures.

The last section of the Old Testament is prophecy; books of varying lengths written by many of God's prophets who lived in Old Testament times. There is a little narrative history included in some of these books, but they are mostly comprised of predictions of future events along various timelines, including both near-term events and prophecies of the end of the world. The writings of the prophets are not the only prophecies in the Old Testament. They are found in every book, including the poetry and law sections. One particularly notable prophecy found throughout the Old Testament describes the coming of a special prophet who will be extremely close to God, sent to help the Jews. He will save the people from their sins and end up ruling over all Israel as a righteous king. This special prophet is referred to as *The Messiah* (or *The Christ*, which means the same thing in Greek). Believers in Judaism are still looking forward to their promised Messiah.

Let us now examine the claims of the Old Testament under our four-point filter.

1. Does it make Logical Sense? Overall, the Old Testament of the Bible is quite a logical story – but only given the premise of an all-powerful God who is unrestricted in His ability to work miracles. Fortunately, that premise is established immediately, in the first sentence of the first book. Therefore, none of the miracles in the Bible violate the logic of the premise. One can argue whether or not a man could survive in the belly of a *great fish* for three days, but because the very first sentence of the Bible establishes the existence of a God who could create such a condition instantly upon His will, any such a debate is rendered spurious.

The teaching that the writers of the scriptures were overcome by God's Spirit when they wrote, and were only transcribing God's truth (making God the true author of the Old Testament), is a validly constructed argument. Remember, we have already proved that we were created, and can witness an infinitely large and infinitely small universe right in front of our eyes. In that light, the Old Testament explanation of our creator does resonate as being logically sensible. He exists in an eternal spiritual dimension located outside of time. He created the entire physical dimension. This explanation corroborates our physicists' current theories that time is an entity intertwined with our universe, not existing outside of it.

The history lessons given in the books of the Old Testament corroborate secular historical records, and archeology has only ever further confirmed this. We apparently have an accurate account of history here; in fact, more than secular history can provide. For that reason, some of the Old Testament history has been doubted by skeptics in semi-modern times. Those skeptics have been silenced after new archeologist digs have confirmed those portions of Bible history which were doubted, however (a good example was the discovery of the Assyrian city of Nineveh in the mid 1800's). When new scientific evidence verifies the claims of very old writings, it strengthens the overall credibility of those writings. Consequently, we can find no conflicts or contradictions of logic in the Old Testament.

2. Is Creation Explained? Yes: God created the universe by willing it to happen. He created all the physical properties of earth, and all the animals living on it, by *speaking* them into existence. God created the first man *out of the dust of the earth*. If these explanations seem incredulous, one need only back up to the first sentence of the Bible again to perceive that they follow the presumption of the eternal existence of an all-powerful, all-knowing God who created the physical dimension. Every facet of that physical dimension is subject to obeying His every whim. This is what the text tells us. It may be difficult to understand the implications of this presumption, and impossible to grasp the scope of it all, but there is no violation of logic here.

It's important to appreciate that the Old Testament gives a rational explanation of existence. We are asked to accept the notion of the preexistence of God, the eternally existing creator, who can do anything He wishes. The very elements which construct our physical universe obey His commands. It is a much more satisfying explanation than just taking for granted the existence of the physical dimension, especially in light of the fact that we have already conclusively disproven the theory of spontaneous generation of life followed by evolution of species on planet earth. We know we were created – protein cells, DNA, and all – so whoever did it must be pretty darn impressive indeed.

God is explained to be both *omnipresent* and *omnipotent* in the Old Testament. That means He is everywhere at once, knows everything, and possesses unrestricted power. He knows every thought of every person alive at all moments, and is aware of what every animal on earth is doing at all times; where every worm is wiggling, and what every ant is doing. He can see the future as clearly as the past and present. He cannot be surprised. Not only is nothing impossible for Him, nothing is even difficult for Him. In this respect, we do see some elements of panentheism in the nature of the Jewish God. In panentheism, however, God is not typified as a personal, knowable God; He is more like *the force* in Star Wars. By contrast, in the Old Testament God is described as having the attributes of a person, complete with a unique personality. We are told He loves us and seeks to have an active relationship with us. The scriptures even state that man was *created in His own image*, which is food for interesting thought.

3. Is the Old Testament a truth which is available for everyone, and is it beneficial for believers? This is an interesting point to consider. The Jews are revealed as *God's chosen people* in the Old Testament. Does that mean nobody else was invited to have fellowship with God?

No. Before the Hebrews even existed, God sought out relationships with virtuous people (such as Able, Enoch, and Noah). There were prophets of God present in other cultures as well. One interesting example is the story of *Balaam*, a prophet of God who lived in a nation that would soon be one of the bordering countries of Israel, and thus certain to become an enemy of them at one time or another. The prophet Jonah was sent to Nineveh, the great city in Assyria, to deliver a warning message to them. The Assyrians were enemies of Israel, yet God had mercy on them when they repented at Jonah's warning.

God did instruct the Jews to utterly destroy every man, woman, and child during the conquest of the Promised Land, but that was justified by the exceptionally wicked practices of those peoples, which included burning their babies alive as sacrifices to their idols.

The descendants of Abraham were chosen to be the ones who would receive God's law, and they were to follow it. This was specifically designed so they could serve as an example, and other nations would then know *there was a true God in Israel*. As it turned out, the Jews were hardly worthy of such an honor. Many Bible teachers have speculated the Jews were specially chosen because of their stubborn and foolish nature, to show God is willing to extend the branch of salvation to even the most difficult to reach.

Foreigners were allowed to reside in ancient Israel, but were expected to keep the Jewish laws if they chose to live there. One intriguing Old Testament story is told in the book of *Ruth*, which is about a Moabite woman who became godly, moved to Israel, and ended up being King David's great grandmother. The Old Testament contains amazing genealogical lists; one can trace some of the later prophets all the way back to the very first man, Adam. Included in those lineages are some prominent non-Jewish figures.

Converting to Judaism today, however, is an impractical notion for non-Jews, for the most part. Being Jewish is a cultural heritage more than a religion these days. The majority of Jews are now professed atheists. It is boggling that the Jewish people have not been assimilated as a race during these last 2,000 years, as well as during the prior time when they were captives in Babylon and Assyria. No other people have ever been so scattered and yet retained their identity. Chalk it up to anti-Semitism and the propensity of Jewish people to keep to themselves, if you will.

There is nothing in the Old Testament which limits any of the laws, historical teachings, prophecies, or poetry to the Jewish people. Quite the contrary, there are passages which reveal that God is interested in the spiritual welfare of all humans on earth. It would appear the Jews were simply chosen as a messenger to the world for God. Any who choose to seek Him with their whole heart, the Old Testament scriptures teach us, will find Him – and there is no restriction mentioned on a person's culture or nationality. The benefits of doing so include blessings from our creator in this life, as well as in the spiritual dimension which follows this life. So, the Old Testament does promise benefits to all who believe and seek to follow God's laws, regardless of national origin.

4. Does the Old Testament offer demonstrable proof of itself? The God of the Bible apparently knew how skeptical we humans would be. While some of the people living in Old Testament times were first-hand witnesses to awesome miracles from God, many who were not eyewitnesses to such events had no inclination to believe those miracles actually happened. Even just a few generations removed from the exodus in Egypt were enough to create doubt over the details of the story. In fact, many of the very same generation, who themselves witnessed the exodus, turned and rebelled against God in their lifetimes. This is all part of the text. What then could the Old Testament possibly offer as proof of its truth to those of us living today?

The prophecy section of the Old Testament claims to be that proof. These 17 books were written by 16 different prophets (Jeremiah wrote two of the books). The writings mainly consist of predictions of future events, most of which are said to have already occurred, and exactly in the manner predicted. The predictions which have not occurred are said to still be pending fulfillment. God is recorded in several places of the Old Testament as intentionally informing us of future events for the specific purpose of providing us with proof of His deity. For example, there is a passage in Isaiah in which God describes himself as *declaring the end from the beginning, and from ancient times the things that are not yet done.* Also in Isaiah, God actually challenges the idols and the false prophets to do the same, saying: *Let them bring them forth, and show us what will happen, let them show the former things, what they be, that we may consider them, and know the latter end of them; or declare us things for to come. Show the things that are to come hereafter, that we may know that ye are gods.*

At the very least, those statements beckon our intellect, demanding further inspection. If specific prophecies were told far in advance, which would be impossible to foresee without divine knowledge, it would constitute demonstrable proof for any reasonable requirements of logic. The only questions would then be whether we could verify that the prophecies were indeed written well in advance, and if they were detailed enough about unforeseeable events to rule out the possibility of chance fulfillment. This is why the prophecies must be specific. Vague prophecies, such as those of Nostradamus, are unimpressive, as one is free to interpret and apply them any way one sees fit. We need names, dates, and places.

The book of Daniel gives such astonishing prophecies of future events that Bible critics have been forced to accuse the book of being written sometime after 70 AD, instead of around 539 BC where scholars and secular history place the date of the writing. Daniel was a prophet of the Babylonian captivity, according to the scriptures (and also according to the words of Jesus in the New Testament). This was during the time of Babylon's existence as the first world empire. In Daniel's writings, he accurately predicted the subsequent conquering of Babylon by the Medo-Persian Empire, which happened in his own lifetime. He then went on to predict the Grecian Empire conquering the Medes and Persians, the subsequent splitting of the Grecian empire into four kingdoms after Alexander the Great would die, followed by the Roman Empire conquering the world. Daniel also predicted the destruction of the temple in Jerusalem and subsequent scattering of Israel which was fulfilled in 70 AD. These prophecies were so specific and so remarkable that you can see the problems the critics have with the book of Daniel.

There are no less amazing prophecies found in the book of Isaiah, which was written around 725 BC, more than 100 years before the Babylonian captivity. Not only did Isaiah accurately predict the Babylonian conquest of Judah, he also predicted their conquering of many other nations with uncanny accuracy. Even more astounding, he predicted the subsequent Medo-Persian conquering of Babylon, and gave the actual name of the Mede king, Cyrus, who would free the Jews to return to their homeland. When this prophecy was written, the Medes were a nomadic tribe and the thought of them becoming a world power was laughable. While not in scripture, it is traditionally thought in Hebrew culture that Daniel showed Cyrus the Isaiah scroll (written nearly 200 years before) which predicted the conquering and mentioned his very name, and this was so impressive that it played a role in Cyrus's decision to free the Jews. These prophecies naturally give the Bible critics another problem – an even more difficult one than the book of Daniel, because many verifiable secular historical records (among them the discovery of the Dead Sea scrolls) place the date of Isaiah's writings when they were supposed to have taken place. The result is a theory that there are actually two writers named Isaiah whose writings were blended into the one book, with the incredible prophecies being written by an Isaiah who lived after the fact.

It should be noted that the only reasoning behind the critics' theories of two Isaiah's and the fraudulent dating of the book of Daniel is their miraculous accuracy in predicting wholly unforeseeable events. The critics have no actual evidence to support these theories, other than the "obvious impossibility" of anybody being able to foretell these unlikely future events so precisely. Therefore, their arguments are logically flawed – especially since there are some secular historical records which corroborate the Biblical timelines for these writings, and especially since we are applying logic to seek a religious truth with an unbiased viewpoint (while knowing we have already proved creation).

Even if we were to dismiss the books of Daniel and Isaiah altogether, we can still find specifically conclusive prophecies in the rest of the books of the prophets. Many of the remaining Old Testament prophets' books predict the future conquering of the northern kingdom by Assyria and/or the future sacking of Jerusalem by Babylon (although often referred to as simply *a great nation from the north*), some of them hundreds of years in advance and well before Babylon was any kind of world power. That alone is specific and convincing. In addition, Jeremiah accurately predicted the Babylonian captivity would last seventy years, and his writings are secularly verified as having been penned in the years immediately preceding the Babylonian invasions.

As already mentioned, the books of the prophets are not the only places prophecy is found in the Old Testament. As far back as the books of Moses, inspired predictions are made, including the future conquering and scattering of the Jews should they neglect God and start worshipping idols. In order to dismiss all of the convincing Old Testament prophecies as having been fraudulently dated, one would need to dismiss nearly every book in the Old Testament – and there is just too much supporting secular history of them for that. The prophecies have been specific, not of a vague nature, and pin pointedly accurate for events which were impossible to foresee. We have no choice but to conclude the Old Testament has provided satisfying, demonstrable proof of its truth.

The Old Testament has passed our four-point filter, which we first established as the only means of arriving at a logical and undeniable truth. We have, therefore, discovered religious truth. We now know about our creator, who He is, His nature and attributes, how and when He created the earth, and have an explanation for our own existence as well as that of the universe.

What's left for us to do? Do we convert to Judaism now, close up shop and get on with our lives? Not quite yet. There are several other religions which accept (or at least incorporate) Old Testament teachings, the largest of which are Christianity and Islam. We now need to investigate those to discover if there is something more to the truth. The Old Testament did promise a messiah, so we want to go see what these other religions who utilize the Old Testament may have to add, using our same four-point filter to analyze their claims. The most logical place to visit next is the oldest and most widely practiced of these religions, which is Christianity by a longshot. Christians claim the New Testament is a further revealing of God's word, and in fact is a fulfillment of Old Testament prophecy. So, let's start there.

New Testament Analysis

The Old Testament was written in Hebrew, but the New Testament was written in Greek during the time of the early Roman Empire, being as Greek had successfully become the primary language in the Mediterranean region during the time of the Grecian Empire. The New Testament consists of 27 individual "books" written by at least eight different men (the authorship of the book of Hebrews is debatable among scholars, but most feel it was written by the apostle Paul). These writings all occurred within the same century.

The New Testament has four sections:

• **The Gospels**

• **Early Church History** (the book of Acts)

• **The Epistles**

• **End Times Prophecy** (the book of Revelation)

The Gospels are the first four books of the New Testament and are supposedly first-hand accounts of the life and ministry of Jesus, from four different perspectives. Each was written as an eyewitness account by one of his disciples. All four Gospels record miracles performed by Jesus, most of which were healing the sick, blind, crippled, and demon-possessed. There are several other types of miracles recorded as well, including turning water into wine, walking on the sea, and miraculously multiplying a few small fish and several loaves of bread into enough food to feed a crowd of thousands.

Each Gospel records the execution of Jesus at the hands of the Romans, instigated by the Jewish religious leaders of the time. Each Gospel records the subsequent miraculous resurrection of Jesus from the dead, and his ascendance into heaven before the eyes of his apostles. Jesus asserted he was both the Son of God and the promised messiah of the Hebrew Scriptures. He taught that he would return one day to establish the kingdom of God upon the earth, and at that time fulfill the remainder of the prophecies about the messiah.

Two of the Gospels give accounts of his miraculous birth, being born of a virgin, which fulfilled two specific Old Testament prophecies about the messiah.

The book of Acts records the creation and early history of the Christian church after Jesus ascended to heaven. Before he ascended, he gave his followers the great commission to take the *message of the gospel* to the entire world. Jesus promised to send his disciples the Holy Spirit as a helper. This occurred in grandiose fashion several days later, in Jerusalem, with such miraculous conviction that thousands of bystanders were converted to Christianity that day, and the church was born. The first church in Jerusalem operated much like a commune, as a way to protect the members from persecution.

Before the Holy Spirit came and empowered the apostles, they were depicted as being fairly helpless and made many mistakes (including bickering among themselves) as is recorded in the Gospels. After the Holy Spirit came upon them in the book of Acts, they became bold, eloquent, sure of themselves, and much more powerful. Some of the apostles acquired the ability to heal disease and cast out demons, while others acquired the gift of prophecy. Apostles soon began travelling to different regions, spreading the news about Jesus and preaching the message of the gospel. They successfully established additional churches in parts of Asia and Europe, in spite of heavy persecution from both the Jewish religious authorities and the Romans.

The message of the gospel is this: The primary purpose of Jesus' first coming was to serve as a sacrifice for the sins of the world. His execution was, in actuality, arranged by God and intentional. Man needed a savior. Jesus was the son of God, God incarnate, and as such was the only person capable of living a sinless life. His torture and execution paid the price for man's sins. All who now believe and sincerely ask forgiveness of their sins through Jesus, and consequently become his follower, will have their sins forgiven and inherit eternal life with God in a spiritual paradise.

Much of the latter half of the book of Acts is about Paul, who was converted to Christianity through a miraculous act of Jesus communicating directly to him. His conversion was staggering to witness, because Paul had been one of the most dedicated persecutors of Christians, championing their imprisonment and execution. He was also one of the most educated men in Israel. Eventually, he assumed the position of the twelfth apostle (they lost one when Judas betrayed Jesus) and became the most prominent evangelist in the group. Many of the additional churches which sprang up were the direct result of Paul's efforts.

The epistles are a collection of letters which were written by the apostles to the first Christian churches. Most of them were written by Paul. They contain instructions on how Christians should live, how the churches should operate, warnings against false teachings, encouragement, rebuking where needed, prophecies, explanations of doctrinal positions, and further revelations about Jesus. Much of Christian church doctrine (even today) is derived from the epistles.

The book of Revelation was written by the apostle John and is the recording of a prophetic vision he supposedly experienced while exiled on the Greek island of Patmos. John lived the longest of all the apostles. The book begins with seven letters to seven specific churches which are dictated by Jesus to John in the vision. Many Bible expositors teach that those letters hold significant symbolic meaning for all ages, in addition to their literal correspondence at the time.

The vision continues with John taken to a heavenly scene where he witnesses future events leading to the return of Jesus to the earth. Many of these events are described symbolically and can be difficult to interpret into literal meaning, especially for new Bible students. It is very clear, however, that the events are descriptions of God's wrath being unleashed upon the earth in His final judgments upon sinful, unrepentant man in the years preceding the return of Jesus. The judgments are quite horrible and include plagues, wars, famine, and contamination of the environment.

It is during this period that the devil gains complete control of the world's governments, through a prodigy who is commonly known as *the anti-Christ*.

Also during this period, John witnesses several events that take place in heaven for which the Christian church is present. This includes a ceremony marking the beginning of the judgment period upon the earth, and a wedding feast where Jesus is joined with his church (referred to as *the marriage supper of the lamb*).

Jesus returns to the earth – with a great number of his followers in tow – just after a devastating war takes place, which culminates in a battle in Israel referred to as the *battle of Armageddon*. That battle occurs in the valley of Armageddon, an actual physical location still on the map today. Jesus puts an end to the wars and plagues and creates paradise-like conditions on the earth for his kingdom, which lasts for 1,000 years. At the end of the 1,000 year reign of Christ, the final judgment day occurs, where unrepentant sinners are cast into an eternal hell along with the devil and all his demons. Heaven and earth are then destroyed, a new heaven and a new earth are created, and the saved live happily ever after with the Lord in paradise.

The Christian church holds the books of the New Testament as inspired writings, just as the Old Testament books are considered to be. Christians believe the writers of the New Testament were overcome by the Holy Spirit when they wrote, making God the actual author of the entire Bible.

Let us now examine the claims of the New Testament under our four-point filter.

1. Does it make Logical Sense? If the Old Testament is first accepted as a valid prequel, The New Testament is indeed a logical following. It does not attempt to refute the Old Testament, but to fulfill many of its important prophecies. The law section of the Old Testament is superseded, however, with the grace of God that is revealed in the New Testament. The word *testament* actually means *covenant* by archaic definition, which is why the New Testament is also referred to as *the new covenant*. Man has proven himself incapable of keeping a set of rules. The Mosaic Law revealed the heart of God, and how He would have His people to live, but much of the literal application was part of the *Abrahamic covenant*, which the New Testament classifies as having been just between God and Israel. In any case, Israel failed to keep up their end of the bargain. Jesus came with a new covenant, available for everyone.

Jesus validated the Old Testament in his teachings, but gave just two commands for his followers, which he said encompassed all of the law of God: *Love God with all your heart, soul, mind, and strength*; and *love your neighbor as yourself.* It is acknowledged in the New Testament, however, that we will fail even with a short list of laws like that. Therefore, it is the heart of man God is concerned with, the humbling of oneself before God and the acceptance of the provision which God made for the atonement of one's sin. The apostle Paul compared life as a race in one of his epistles and encouraged Christians to keep running the race *with their eyes on the prize.* The real purpose of the law, Paul wrote, was to convict us of sin and point us towards the need for a savior.

The logic of the New Testament is valid and presents no conflicts with Old Testament teachings.

2. Is Creation Explained? Yes, because the New Testament accepts the Old Testament history as truth, including the account of creation. The only further revelation of creation in the New Testament is that of God's plural nature; having manifested Himself into several centers of consciousness in the persons of the Father, Son, and Holy Spirit. The three parts to the one God is not considered polytheistic, however, as the three persons of the Godhood retain a unity of each being a component of the one God. This actually sheds light on some plural references God made of Himself in the Old Testament, such as in Genesis during creation when he said: *let **us** make man in **our** image.*

3. Is the New Testament a truth which is available for everyone, and is it beneficial for believers? Yes. The great commission Jesus gave the apostles was to spread the message of the gospel to the entire world. John's Gospel states that *God sent His Son into the world so that the world through him might be saved.* Jesus taught that there were two paths in life; one leading to destruction which is wide and heavily travelled, and one leading to salvation which is narrow and lightly travelled. Jesus also taught of an eternal hell for those rejecting God and His plan of forgiveness. The benefit offered by the teachings of the New Testament is nothing less than saving oneself from the eternal hell and gaining an eternal paradise. There can be no greater possible benefit, and the gospel is available to all.

4. Does the New Testament offer demonstrable proof of itself? The prophecies in the New Testament are of events which still lie in the future, or are too vague to be able to rule out chance fulfillment. For example, Jesus predicted that in the end times there would be *wars and rumors of wars, and kingdom would rise against kingdom.* The special kind of *kingdom rising against kingdom* war is thought by many to have been fulfilled by the two world wars in the 20th century, but is not specific enough to be demonstrable proof of fulfillment, since there have been continuous wars between countries throughout all of history. So, the New Testament does not prove itself in the manner which the Old Testament was able to (not yet, anyway) through specific prophecies of future events that were impossible to foresee.

There is something else to be examined, however. The New Testament claims to be the fulfillment of Old Testament prophecies. Because we have already proven the Old Testament as religious truth, should the New Testament be able to prove itself as a fulfillment of those prophecies, this would provide logical, conclusive proof of its truth as well. Such a conclusion must be drawn from irrefutable evidence, however.

Before we look at this, it is important to fully comprehend just where we stand in our investigation. We have logically proven creation. Spontaneous generation of life followed by evolution has been conclusively disproven, and admitted to be impossible even by leading evolutionary scientists. There is no alternative but creation. Knowing creation to be a truth, we then investigated the teachings of the Old Testament and found them to be religious truth due to their accurate foretelling of impossible to foresee future events, in a specific manner, and by many different writers whose lives and timeframes have been historically verified by outside sources. We know the Old Testament is accurate and true, and we know a messiah was promised to Israel in it.

The New Testament records the life of Jesus and the beginnings of the Christian church, and claims Jesus was the promised messiah of the Old Testament. Therefore, if that can be proven, then we will know the New Testament is indeed a continuation of the religious truth we are seeking.

There were over 360 prophecies regarding the coming of the messiah in the Old Testament. Christians claim that Jesus fulfilled every one of them in one manner or another. Of the 360+ messianic prophecies, 109 of them are said to be impossible to have been fulfilled by any person other than Jesus. These include things such as his virgin birth, the special star in the sky that shone over his birthplace, and details about his execution.

There is a law in mathematics known as the *law of compound probabilities*. It basically determines what the odds are of a specific series of events happening by chance. The more of them which happen, the greater the odds are against it. When applied to a series of events in which each event by itself is considered unlikely, the odds quickly become astronomical before you reach even a dozen of such events happening. Assuming the life of Jesus is recorded correctly in the Gospels – and there is no rational reason to assume otherwise – it is so far beyond mathematically impossible for Jesus to be a chance fulfillment that it is not worthy of consideration.

Now, it is reasonable to step back and ponder whether or not the entire New Testament could have been a clever fabrication designed at messianic prophecy fulfillment. The books of the New Testament were, after all, all written within one generation. We do know that the Jesus of the Bible did in fact live, right at the time the Bible reports, from secular historical records (all one needs to do is an internet search for *secular evidence of Jesus Christ* to read these accounts – some of those secular records even include accounts of his resurrection from the dead). So, at the very least, we know Jesus lived.

Knowing the person of Jesus did actually live at the time the New Testament places him, we have a difficult time discrediting the Bible as a source of evidence about him. There is no logical reason to, especially since the Bible's historical accounts about everything else have always proven to be accurate. It is also worth considering that Christians in the first century A.D. were literally risking their lives for their belief, and thousands of them were willing to be executed rather than renounce their faith. These were the people of Jesus' own generation and the following generation, ones who lived very close to the accounts given in the Gospels and who were converts of the first Christian churches. Humans do not normally give up their lives for a belief that they know is a falsehood, so it is a strong testimony that these first generations were willing to die a martyr's death for Christ.

Many would insist that the miracles recorded in the Bible should be discredited as evidence, based on the assumption that miracles are not possible in science. This logic is flawed, however, in an investigation of religious truth. We have already proved creation, so our entire existence is a "miracle" by science standards. In addition, there are many modern-day medical miracles on record in which people diagnosed with terminal diseases were inexplicably completely healed after groups of Christians prayed for them. To dismiss the miracles of the Bible, but accept the historical records, is a difficult position to defend as anything other than an emotional reaction rooted in a biased attitude.

Nevertheless, even if we neglect the events in the life of Christ which constitute miracles (such as his virgin birth), we are still left with too many such events for chance fulfillment. Consider just the following:

• Born in Bethlehem

• From King David's lineage

• Lived briefly in Egypt

• Raised in Nazareth

• Entered Jerusalem triumphantly on a donkey colt

• Rejected by the religious authorities

• Betrayed by a friend for 30 pieces of silver

• Hung on a cross

• Offered vinegar to drink while dying

• Died with criminals

• No bone was broken

• His side was pierced

• Buried with the rich

• Lots were cast for his clothes

Those 14 events alone, which were all prophecies in the Old Testament about the messiah, are much more than enough to make chance fulfillment a mathematical impossibility according to the law of compound probability. In fact, the chances of just the first eight of those events occurring (in the life of one person) has been calculated by mathematicians to be about one chance in 10 to the 150th power, far beyond the 10 to the 50th power which is considered mathematically impossible.

It is also worth noting that one particular prophecy, in the book of Daniel, accurately foretold the exact day the messiah would be riding into Jerusalem on a donkey colt, and Jesus did just that on the foretold date. Now, you'd think that the religious men of the day would have been there waiting for him, having had that knowledge ahead of time – but they weren't, which says something about their true motives.

It simply must be concluded that Jesus was the promised messiah of the Old Testament from the prophecies his life fulfilled. There is no logical, rational, or mathematical way to deny this, as the evidence is overwhelming. The New Testament has, therefore, proven itself to be religious truth. It passed our four-point filter. This means the entire Bible is religious truth.

Our work is not yet done, however. There are further claimed revelations which attempt to build on the religious truth of the Bible, in the same manner the New Testament built upon the truth of the Old Testament. We need to examine those. We will then need to see what is left on our list of candidates which could possibly be compatible with our proven religious truth, and investigate those, if any are left. Anything which conflicts can be safely eliminated, as we have already proven the Bible as religious truth, and logic will not allow for contradicting truths.

First, however, we should logically examine the Bible as a whole, to see if there are any further insights to be gained, and to question whether only parts of the Bible could be true.

Consideration of the Bible as a Whole

We have already analyzed both the Old and New Testaments individually. The Old Testament proved itself as religious truth by accurately foretelling future events which were impossible to foresee, hundreds of years in advance in some cases. In the Old Testament, God Himself stated that by prophecy we would know He is the true God. The New Testament also proved itself as religious truth, by fulfilling the most repeated (and most important) prophecy of the Old Testament in a manner which is mathematically undeniable. There are some religions, however, that claim only parts of the Bible are true, and that other parts are fabrications of man. Is this a logical possibility? Could the prophecy portions of the Old Testament be accepted as divinely inspired, seeing as they have proved themselves, but other Biblical texts contain falsehoods or human fantasy?

Let's examine this idea. The prophets of the Old Testament who so impressively predicted the Babylonian captivity far in advance were obviously inspired by God. Those same prophets described God as being omnipresent and omnipotent (all-knowing and all-powerful), but also as a benevolent, merciful, loving father who would forgive His children and cancel the conquests of His people if they would only turn back to Him. Because we have no choice but to believe the writings of those who proved themselves with prophecy, we must also logically accept what they have written about the nature of God.

An all-powerful God who created all life and the entire universe is capable of writing a book. It is ludicrous to suppose otherwise. There are Bible verses which tell us *it is impossible for God to lie*, but we really already know this from logical deduction. A benevolent and loving God would not give His children false information, especially regarding important matters which affect their well-being. Those who believe that parts of the Bible may not be true must not believe in the all-powerful and loving God of the Bible. Such a viewpoint creates a logical contradiction, because the prophets who accurately foretold impossible-to-see future events many years in advance also told us God is all-powerful and loving.

105

The Bible tells us God is everywhere all the time, knows every thought every person has, and can cause any person to do whatever God wills at His whims. There are examples given in the Bible where God caused men to carry out actions which accomplished His will. One notable case in point is the story of Nebuchadnezzar, the king of Babylon who was the first emperor to conquer the known world. God used the king of Babylon to punish other nations, including His own people in Judah. When Nebuchadnezzar became prideful over his accomplishments, God corrected him by making him think he was a cow, resulting in the king having to crawl around eating grass for seven years. Everything Nebuchadnezzar had "accomplished" was only because God had empowered him and willed him to do so.

While we certainly have our own free will, the Bible tells us God is capable of directing our free will in such a way that what we want to do is what God wants us to do, anytime He so chooses. One can never be entirely certain that one's actions are not being fully directed by God. It is in this manner God is able to use men to write His book accurately and with whole truth. It is also in this manner God is able to ensure His book is copied over accurately from generation to generation. To even suggest God's book may have been corrupted by man is laughable in this respect. A person making such a suggestion does not hold a Biblical concept of God. The same prophets who told us of impossible-to-foresee events also assured us that God loves us, is all-knowing and all-powerful, and cannot lie. Under these conditions, it is not possible for any part of the Bible to be false.

A person who believes in the God of the Bible, but also believes the Bible contains falsehoods, must necessarily believe at least one of the following:

• God intentionally put falsehoods in the Bible

• God allowed falsehoods to be written in the Bible (or allowed the Bible to become corrupted at some point)

• God is not powerful enough to keep falsehoods out of the Bible

At least one of the above three must be true if the Bible teaches anything false, even the smallest and most insignificant detail. A person holding such a belief should examine what else they believe about God and look for conflicts of logic. For example, if they believe God is all-powerful, then they have a conflict if they also believe He was unable to keep the Bible from containing falsehoods or becoming corrupted. If they believe He simply did not wish to prevent the Bible from containing false teachings, or didn't care enough to stop it, then they have a conflict if they also believe God is benevolent and loves us. Ultimately, the logic of such beliefs breaks down. One cannot rationally believe in the God of the Bible and reject that same Bible as containing falsehoods.

Likewise, religious beliefs which claim the Bible contains falsehoods but quote certain Bible verses as support for their doctrinal teachings are displaying a sorrowful, obvious contradiction in sound reasoning. To utilize a source which you claim is flawed in an attempt to prove your position is the height of folly.

Compilation and Authority

God used at least 40 men to write the 66 sections of His book. Most scholars place the timespan of the writings to have taken place over more than 1,200+ years, and many place the timespan in excess of 1,500+ years or even longer. The men God used to compose the individual books of the Bible came from diverse backgrounds. Some were fishermen, some were kings, some were shepherds, and some were called from an early age to be priests or prophets. These men lived in different times, grew up in different countries and cultures, and spoke different languages. They came from different classes of society and had different political leanings. To say the Bible originated from a fragmented source would be an understatement.

The Bible was finally compiled in the second and third centuries A.D. by Christian church authorities. Much study went into arriving at the canon of scripture, and only those writings which were thought to be self-evident of their inspired nature were included. One can certainly argue about whether those men correctly identified and properly arranged the inspired writings if one does not view God as being powerful (or caring) enough to direct their efforts, but such a notion is irrational based on what the proven prophets of the Old Testament have told us about God.

Once the Bible had been compiled, it began to prove itself in new and unexpected ways. The first method in which it did this was by the harmony of the Bible itself, and the unity of its theme. One could start at the beginning and just read it as one reads a book, and be delighted with its natural progression and enlightenment. Considering the writings' fragmented origins, this would seem an impossible result without divine direction in its entire creation. Keep in mind the men who wrote the books of the Bible were only composing their own God-directed writings during their individual lifetimes, and had no idea they were contributing to any kind of a larger work.

Another new way the Bible began to prove itself was through the transformation of those who read it. Individuals with no particular beliefs would read it out of curiosity and find they believed in its teachings as they went. Their very lives would often be transformed through the act of reading God's word. This is not the only supernatural experience people have reported from Bible study. Believers often claim they find answers to their everyday problems in unexpected places when they open their Bible for their daily reading. There are Bible verses which offer an explanation for this, among them one which states that *the Word of God is a living, breathing entity, sharper than any two-edged sword.* Many people have reported experiences that could be described as borderline-miraculous while reading the scriptures.

Perhaps the most remarkable method in which the Bible proves itself is the inability of a person to exhaust oneself of it. Any other book it seems, when read often enough, eventually becomes stale and depleted of satisfactory stimuli. This is not the case with the Bible. Many people read it perpetually, starting again at the beginning as soon as they finish it, over and over for much of their lives. Those who perform this regimen, even elderly church pastors who have read the Bible dozens of times, often report that each time they reread the same passages new meanings and insights are imparted to them. That so many people can testify of this phenomenon sheds light on the verse about the Bible being a living thing, not just a book. Somehow the words from God are far more nourishing and attentive to us than any words which are merely from man.

The question of Bible authority is asked by some. They demand evidence that the writings of the Bible are any more authoritative than the writings used as scriptural sources for other religions and belief systems. I do believe we have already answered this, but let us recap in a way that specifically addresses these concerns.

Using an unbiased frame of mind, we deduced that the most logical place to begin a search for religious truth was with the oldest religious beliefs that are still practiced today. It makes sense that a loving creator who wanted us to have the truth would make that truth available to every generation of humans, right from the beginning. It is illogical (and disturbing) to suggest that a loving creator would hold back religious truth for many generations, allowing millions of people to live and die over thousands of years without having access to it. A benevolent God would be there for His people from the get-go. This line of reasoning led us to the Old Testament first, which did prove itself as truth upon our analysis. This is a logical finding if you think about it. If all of the oldest religious texts were found to be logically flawed, it would make proving later-written religious texts a much more difficult task, as we would then also need a satisfying explanation as to why the truth was hidden from man for so long – and it is difficult to imagine a satisfactory answer to that query.

It is true that there are other very old religious texts still in existence and still adhered to in some eastern cultures. We logically assigned the investigation of those a low priority, however, being as their teachings lack urgency, do not provide explanations of creation, and whether they offer any real benefits to believers is questionable to a western mindset. They were not a logical place to begin our research from a work-efficiency standpoint. Now that we have logically proven the Bible as truth, we have automatically eliminated these very old eastern religious texts because they sharply contradict what we already know to be true. The Bible tells us God is not an impersonal and unknowable force, and the concept of reincarnation directly conflicts with what Jesus taught (Jesus having been mathematically proven to be the messiah promised by the prophetically-proven Old Testament).

It is obvious from every application of logic that the entire Bible is God's book, and as such it must be inerrant and infallible.

Further Revelations and Bible Modifications

Since the compilation of the Bible, many alternative religious viewpoints have arisen which claim to be a further revelation built upon the foundation laid by the Bible. This is not an illogical concept in and of itself, so it cannot be immediately dismissed. We need to examine these claims and teachings, using what we already know to be true as the measuring standard. If any conflicts with the teachings of the Bible are found, we must be highly suspicious and demand that they prove themselves. We have already discovered truth, and cannot readily compromise it based on unsubstantiated claims.

It is true that the New Testament revelation of God's grace supplanted at least some of the Old Testament law. Therefore, the notion that further revelations could supplant New Testament teachings may seem consistent with that process, at least on the surface. While examining these claims, we must keep in mind the manner in which the New Testament revelation occurred. It was a fulfillment of Old Testament

112

prophecy, and it solved a problem left by the Old Testament, that of man's inability to keep the law of God. Any further revelations should therefore follow in like manner, proving themselves as the fulfillment of Bible prophecy and solving any remaining problems the New Testament has left us with.

One foreseeable difficulty in accomplishing that will be in convincing us there is still a problem to be solved, being as the New Testament has a sense of completeness about it. Indeed, where the Old Testament left off it essentially told us to *stay tuned because more is coming*, while the New Testament tells us we have the complete truth and warns of false teachers coming after it. The fact that the entire Bible reads through with a unity of theme and feeling of completeness becomes part of its testimony, so any further revelations would need to stay in that harmony and not present unresolved conflicts.

The Bible did in fact warn that false teachers would come and deceive many with new, erroneous religious doctrines. The Bible told us to inspect any new teachings using the basic message of the gospel as the measuring standard, and also the fact that Jesus was the Old Testament messiah *who had come in the flesh*. Any new teachings which deny Jesus as the messiah come in the flesh, or which distort the central message of the gospel (that man is a sinner who needs a savior and God provided that savior, His own Son who died on the cross for our sins, so all who accept him and believe will be saved by God's grace alone) are to be flat-out rejected as false. The message of the gospel is the nucleus of the Bible, the all-important aspect which makes it possible for sinners to be reconciled to God. There is just no messing with that.

As it turns out, while these Bible-modification religions vary widely in doctrinal teachings, they tend to have one thing in common: distorting the message of the gospel. This is not surprising, because the Bible specifically warns of it. The Bible teaches us about the devil, our powerful enemy who is seeking to destroy us. The only truly important thing for our salvation is the message of the gospel; therefore it makes perfect sense that this is the part which is always distorted. If you don't mind that, you can find a tremendous assortment of alternative beliefs, something for everybody, like a 31-flavor ice cream store. The enemy doesn't particularly care which way we are lost, only that we become lost. It is the gospel which must be denied for that to happen. Some way or another, a false religion must teach you that Jesus didn't really die for your sins. One popular way of accomplishing this is to refuse to acknowledge we are sinners in the first place (and in so doing deny the existence of an eternal hell); another is to deny the crucifixion and replace it with a works-based salvation.

In the New Testament book of Galatians, the apostle Paul makes a prophetic warning about false teachers who would come *preaching another gospel*, and pronounces a curse on those false teachers *even if they be angels*. As we will see in a moment, several popular alternative religions have actually started

114

with an angel supposedly visiting somebody and giving a "revelation" which conflicts with the gospel.

Islam

The second largest religion on planet earth is Islam, which began when an Arab man named Muhammad was visited by an angel preaching another gospel. This happened early in the seventh century, more than 400 years after the Bible was first compiled. The angel was supposedly Gabriel, a noteworthy figure from the Bible.

The revelation was given to Muhammad verbally and he was able to memorize it, apparently with divine help. He relayed it to his contemporaries and began to gain followers. After a while, many of his followers would memorize all of the teachings as well. After the prophet's death, some of his followers wrote the teachings down, which are known in their entirety as *the Quran*. It is an impressive testimony to this religion that even today there are Muslims who have memorized the entire Quran, which is quite a mental feat.

Over the centuries, many offshoots of Islam have come into existence. There are now dozens of varieties of Islam practiced, many of which teach conflicting doctrine with one another. Common to all of them, however, is the holding of the Quran as a sacred and authoritative religious text. Interestingly, Muslims do not dispute the Bible except in cases where the Quran conflicts with it, and of course it conflicts with it sharply in regards to the message of the gospel (otherwise Muslims would be Christians). Islam is, therefore, a belief that the Quran came to supplant the New Testament in certain critical issues.

So, Muslims believe some parts of the Bible are true, but not other parts. We have already discussed the illogic of such a belief. In Islam, this is justified by the concept of a further revelation supplanting the prior truth. Unfortunately, the further revelation contradicts historical events given in the prior truth, which infers that God allowed outright falsehoods in His original book. Christians logically hold that an all-powerful, loving God could not have done such a thing (which may shed some light on why the God is not depicted as being particularly loving and benevolent in the Quran).

The Quran denies the plural nature of God and states that Jesus was only a man, not a deity. The Quran does refer to Jesus as a prophet, however. This creates the biggest logical contradiction in Islam. A prophet by definition is one who reveals divine truth. Jesus claimed to be a deity, the Son of God, one with the Father in fact. Therefore, he cannot be a prophet unless he is what he claimed to be. The Quran would have done logic a much better service by condemning Jesus as a false prophet.

The Quran states that Jesus did not die on the cross for our sins. In fact, it states that he did not die on the cross at all, but was taken to heaven alive. Islam teaches a works-based salvation instead; one's good

116

works should outweigh one's sins, which is sometimes depicted by the symbol of a scale in Islamic imagery.

The Quran portrays Israel as an enemy of Islam. This is a blatant (and dangerous) contradiction of the Old Testament teaching that *those who bless Israel will be blessed and those who curse Israel will be cursed.*

It is a fascinating tragedy that what they believe about their salvation really does not conflict with the Bible, because Muslims do not profess to know whether they are saved. They can only hope to pass God's judgment upon their death, based on their good works while they were alive. This is not an unbiblical belief! The Bible teaches that all non-Christians will stand in judgment before God. However, it also teaches that it is impossible for us to do enough good works to make up for our sin. God's standard is just too high. We cannot have any sin at all on that side of the scale if we are to be saved. Jesus himself (a prophet according to Islam) stated that if one hopes to be saved by their works, then their works must *exceed* those of the Pharisees, the religious zealots of Jesus' day who dedicated their entire lives to keeping the Mosaic Law. If they couldn't do it, it seems unlikely anyone can.

According to the gospel, God arranged for our sin to be completely forgiven through the sacrifice of His son. We are free to accept or reject the sacrifice. If we accept it, there is no judgment upon us because Jesus was already judged for our sin on the cross. If we reject the sacrifice, we will stand in judgment, and the

Bible flat-out warns that we have no hope of passing that judgment. Yet, this is precisely where the hope of Islam lies, in attempting to pass that judgment. Refusing the free offer of forgiveness through Christ is not wise. The New Testament book of Hebrews puts it like this: ...*how shall we escape if we ignore such a great salvation?*

Islam claims to offer prophecy in the Quran as evidence of its truth. Those prophecies, however, are either too vague to be able to rule out chance fulfillment or were repeated prophecies from the Bible. For example, there is a prophecy about men being *betrayed by their skin* in the end times, and the claim is that fingerprint technology fulfilled that prophecy. This is much too vague to be logically convincing. The one impressive prophecy in the Quran is that of Israel being gathered again into their Biblical homeland in the last days, which has indeed now occurred – but this prophecy was simply repeated from the Bible, so was not an original teaching in the Quran.

Christian evangelism efforts do see some success in Islamic regions, despite the inherent danger involved. (While mosques are popping up all over western society, Christian evangelists are still put to death in many Islamic countries today.) Some Muslims will logically accept the message of the gospel, and, in doing so, tend to experience a sense of relief, as one whom has just had a great burdened removed. It is an unbiblical stance for Christians to hate Muslims. Though many Muslims do consider Christians to be their enemy, Jesus instructed his followers to love their enemy. Muslims do have a tremendous zeal for God, and thus logically should be fertile ground for Christian evangelism.

Mormonism

In the year 1820, the founding Mormon prophet Joseph Smith was supposedly visited by an angel preaching another gospel, in response to Smith's prayers asking God to show him the one true religion. Joseph Smith didn't need to go through the logical deduction process we did in order to arrive at the truth (which is a real shame); instead, an angel visited him and informed him that none of the world's religions were truth. He was given instructions on where to dig in the ground to find some golden plates with the real religious truth written on them, which he did, and subsequently recorded that truth in writing the Book of Mormon.

Like Muslims, Mormons do not dispute the Bible except in cases where it conflicts with the Book of Mormon. They read from the Bible in their churches at times. Unfortunately, the book of Mormon teaches a fair amount of diametrically opposing doctrine to that which is taught in the Bible, including a very subtle (but wholly destructive) distortion of the message of the gospel. Therefore, Mormonism is found to be guilty of the conspicuous illogic of referencing the Bible as a source of scriptural support while believing that source to be flawed.

119

The Book of Mormon denies the deity of Jesus. It teaches that he was a created being, an angelic creature like Satan. Both Satan and Jesus supposedly presented plans for man's salvation to God; Satan's plan was rejected and Jesus' plan was accepted. This is what caused Satan to rebel, being upset over having lost the salvation-plan competition with Jesus. Obviously, this is a blatant contradiction with Bible teachings, which state that Satan was never interested in man's salvation and is responsible for tempting him into original sin in the first place. Jesus affirmed that *he was a murderer from the beginning* in John's Gospel.

It is interesting that Mormons believe Jesus did die on the cross for our sins. Isn't that the important thing? Doesn't that make Mormons Christians, and saved by gospel standards? The problem, many Christian church authorities argue, is their incorrect concept of who Jesus is. One common objection Christian pastors have with the Mormon view is that "they believe in a different Jesus." Still, it is debatable as to whether having an incorrect concept of the nature of Jesus is enough to invalidate the gospel message. We are incapable of grasping the full scope of God anyway, right?

The real problem with Mormonism is actually more subtle than properly understanding the deity of Christ. By reducing Jesus to the status of a created being, one tends to gravitate towards a position of belief without personal acceptance. The New Testament book of James tells us there is a difference between believing *of* something and believing *in* something, *for even the demons believe and tremble at God's name.* The message of the gospel includes the necessity of repenting from one's sins and accepting Jesus as your savior. To believe he died as the sacrifice for the sins of the world, but neglect to enter into a personal relationship with him, is to tread on dangerous ground from the Christian perspective. Believing Christ died for your sins is one matter, personally receiving Christ and claiming ownership of that sacrifice as payment for your own sin is quite another. As already stated, the difference is subtle – but potentially detrimental.

U.S. presidential candidate Mitt Romney shed some light on this point when he was interviewed by Barbara Walters on a network television show which aired in 2012. The show was about various religious viewpoints on the topic of heaven. Romney assured Barbara that she was going to heaven, without knowing anything about her personal beliefs. Mormons reject the concept of an eternal hell and believe everybody is going to heaven, a teaching in direct opposition with what Jesus taught and what many Old Testament scriptures revealed about hell.

What Mormons are primarily concerned with is *exaltation* to a better position in the afterlife. A typical Mormon will preach the concept of *saved by grace, exalted by works*, in defense of being accused of practicing a works-based salvation. It is a logical reply and accurately represents what they believe. It is also a good debate response which will silence many

121

Christians on the issue, because it is not far removed from New Testament references to the *judgment seat of Christ*, an event that is tantamount to an awards ceremony in heaven for things done on earth.

But, the Bible teaches that there is an eternal hell. The problem with the doctrine that everyone goes to heaven is it makes the doctrine of salvation a moot point. Everybody is going to paradise anyway, so repenting of one's sin and receiving Christ as your Lord and Savior loses its significance – especially if Jesus is not even a deity. Mormons are much more concerned with their exaltation in the afterlife, which they believe they can attain through works in this life. That is where their real passion lies. From a Biblical perspective, taking your salvation for granted and working on your exaltation is putting the cart before the horse. There is a Bible passage in the book of Revelation which indicates the saved will all be throwing their "awards" back to the throne of God anyway. It's your salvation that is important in the Bible. We are told to *work that out with fear and trembling* and to be careful not to abandon our humility.

Although they will not usually publicly admit it, Mormon doctrine teaches that accomplished Mormons will be exalted to godhood one day, eventually becoming equal with the God of the Bible in stature. They believe they can be in charge of their own planet, becoming the god of their own world. The God of the Bible is thus only one such god in a universe full of gods over other planets. What

Mormonism really boils down to is a polytheistic religion that distorts Bible teachings into a dangerous doctrine which primarily serves to fuel self-ambition. Ironically, the Bible tells us (through two Old Testament passages) that this was the very sin which caused Satan to fall from grace; attempting to exalt oneself to equality with God.

Jesus is a Bible character held in high regard in Mormonism, just as he is in Islam. Here again we see a violent breach of logic in that Jesus claimed to be a deity, the Son of God, equal with the Father. Mormonism denies this, while at the same time believing they themselves can become equal with God. Therefore, in reality, they place themselves above Christ, who they relegate to the level of angel, an inferior being. In any case, one cannot logically hold a liar or a lunatic in high regard, and Jesus must be one or the other if he is not who he claimed to be.

While it may not be immediately apparent, upon close examination it is seen that the teachings of Mormonism obliterate – not just supplant – many of the cardinal doctrines of Biblical Christianity. In addition, the illogic of referencing the Bible for scriptural support when the Bible is believed to be flawed is not compatible with sound reasoning. Therefore, we must demand Mormonism prove itself in a demonstrable way before we could consider it as religious truth. It does not even attempt to do this, however. Mormons apparently believe in their religion purely on the basis that it is a good-sounding story, and do not bother to dissect it logically.

Mormonism offers no new prophecies which have proved themselves. The only Biblical prophecy Mormonism evidently fulfills is that of false religions coming and deceiving many, even if they come by an angel.

Christian Science

This one is not really worthy of mention here, other than the fact that they attempt to tag themselves as being Christian. Nothing could be further from the truth. Christian Science denies the atoning sacrifice of Christ, denies the deity of Christ, denies the notion that man is a sinner who needs forgiveness, denies the physical resurrection of Christ, denies the existence of hell, denies the Bible is true, and oh yeah – denies the existence of the physical dimension itself. This religion was started in the mid-1800's by a man and a woman who were subsequently exposed to have been involved in fraudulent activities. Christian Science is primarily concerned with the practice of mental healing, which is a way of "thinking yourself well" when you are sick (based on the notion that since nothing is real, the sickness is not real either). Christian Scientists believe Christ was just a person who got good at the art of mental healing.

At its core, the beliefs are pantheistic – non panentheistic, because they refuse to acknowledge the existence of the physical realm. Obviously, we cannot logically deny the existence of what we see, feel, and hear right in front of us. How an intelligent person could subscribe to such a belief is a mystery that will be explored in the last section of this book.

Bottom line, Christian Science is neither Christian nor science.

Jehovah's Witnesses

The Jehovah's Witnesses are an interesting group of Bible modifiers. Founded in the late 1800's by a man who was later found to be guilty of fraud and perjury when he attempted to sue a detractor for libel in a Canadian court, this North American religion has changed doctrinal positions significantly over the last hundred years. One must admire their ability to be pliable with the ebb and flow of the times, at least, and still be able to boast more than seven million followers worldwide. Jehovah's Witnesses are classified as a Christian denomination (as is Mormonism) by secular sources, but are classified as a non-Christian cult by Christian church authorities (as is Mormonism).

Jehovah's Witnesses deny the existence of hell and the plural nature of God that is revealed in the New Testament. They believe Jesus to be a created being, but a special one who is set above the rest of creation. They do not accept the physical resurrection of Christ, only a spiritual one, and claim Christ has returned to the earth already in "spirit form" and administers his kingdom this very moment through the Watchtower organization. Rather than spend an eternity in hell, JW's believe the non-saved are annihilated. They claim exclusivity on salvation in the current age; only Jehovah's Witnesses can become saved nowadays, and everyone else will be annihilated. This is what makes them a cult (well, that and their cult-like recruiting methods).

They also claim the Bible is true. Now, we have just mentioned a handful of their flagrantly unbiblical beliefs, so you can see the first logical problem. The Bible teaches there is a hell, but the JW's say there is no hell and the Bible is all true. How can such an obvious, severe contradiction of logic be accepted by more than seven million people?

One thing that helps is they had their own version of the Bible translated. Not by Greek and Hebrew scholars, but by hires who were told to bend the scriptures to Watchtower doctrine. In this respect, they have changed words and phrases in appropriate places which would help to lessen the Biblical passages pertaining to the trinity, the deity of Christ, and the existence of hell. The JW's are the only ones who use this version of the Bible, which stands alone among hundreds of translations in many such issues.

Try as they might, even their specially-tweaked version of the Bible was not successful in removing all teachings of hell, the deity of Christ, and the trinity. The JW's are not too concerned about it. First and foremost in the priorities of a Jehovah's Witness is his or her commitment to the Watchtower organization. It is taught to be God's organization on earth and takes precedence even over scripture. In this manner, followers can learn to ignore annoying little quirks in the Bible (even their own special version of it) which contradict the organization's doctrinal teachings.

The most fascinating thing about these folks is they do believe Jesus died on the cross for our sins, and that they are saved by putting their faith and trust in Christ. That *is* the basic message of the gospel. With no fear of hell – and a concept of Jesus which places him one step under God but above all else – is this a dangerous distortion of the gospel, salvation-wise? The jury is still out. One must suppose it depends on the individual, and perhaps on whether their relationship with Christ is placed above their relationship with the Watchtower organization. Therein lays the real danger of this belief system. Is one's faith and trust primarily in Jesus, or in an organization?

We cannot, of course, seriously entertain it as a further revelation of religious truth, being as it is essentially just a doctrinal argument over scripture, and a question of where one places their loyalty. The Watchtower organization has done nothing to offer demonstrable proof that they are God's own company, and the notion that only JW's practice true Christianity is so arrantly unbiblical that it must be rejected as an obvious falsehood.

Rastafarianism

More than just marijuana-infused Bible study, the Rasta movement is a theology with a strong political statement. It arose in Jamaica in the 1930's and made its mark on pop culture when reggae music became popular in the mid-20th century, especially with the international success of musician Bob Marley. Rastafarians believe the Bible for the most part, but have specific (and quite unorthodox) beliefs about end-times prophecy fulfillment. Unfortunately, one of those beliefs is that Jesus has already returned to the earth physically through the act of reincarnation, and has become Haile Selassie I, the former and final Emperor of Ethiopia. When Selassie died in 1975, it really threw a wrench in the Rasta machinery and the movement saw much dissention, even within its own doctrinal teachings. Some Rastafarians try to explain his death by twisting it into other Bible prophecy interpretations; others insist he did not really die. In any case, the Rasta movement has staying power, probably much more due to its strong cultural attraction with young people than the rationale of its doctrine.

What we see here is a trap that many Christian pastors, and even some entire denominations, have fallen into: that of predicting the return of Christ in a specific manner. Jesus taught very strongly that no person would know exactly when he would next come, that it would be a surprise, and that the entire population on earth would witness his final second coming when it happens. He also told us not to believe anyone who said he had already returned to the earth, because when he does return everyone will know it. Some otherwise respectable Bible teachers have ruined their reputations with blown predictions of the return of Christ by certain dates. Such a practice is clearly unbiblical and thus quite unwise. In 1975, the death of the Ethiopian Emperor proved the Rastafarian religion to be a false theology. One can only hope the current practitioners spend more time reading their Bible and less time smoking dope and looking to a dead human king for salvation.

Liberal Christianity

The term *liberal Christianity* is rightfully considered an oxymoron, but we will use it here to identify modern Christian church practices which compromise Biblical teachings with cultural trends. This is really an area of doctrine and interpretation rather than a claimed further revelation or Bible modification, so we won't spend much time on it.

Compromising straightforward Bible teachings in an effort to be viewed as politically correct is a sad breakdown of logic. If we have religious truth, and that religious truth warns us wicked days are coming (as the Bible clearly does), the last thing a church which claims to be Bible-based should be doing is bending their doctrine away from what the Bible teaches in order to be friendly with the wicked culture. Such a practice nullifies the very substance of what is supposedly being taught. It is quite similar in essence to utilizing a source which you claim to be flawed in an attempt to support your position, only in reverse. In this case, the source isn't flawed, but the practices of the church which holds the source to be true violate the teachings of that source. This cheapens the authority of the source in the eyes of the followers.

One such example is the Evangelical Lutheran Church making the decision to allow openly-homosexual pastors in 2009. Similar decisions have been made in the 21st century by the Episcopal and Presbyterian churches, among others. The practice of homosexuality is singled out in both the Old and New Testaments as *an abomination to God.*

Methodist churches have allowed female clergy members for decades now, a practice which the apostle Paul forbade in the New Testament book of I Timothy.

Those are just two examples of blatantly unbiblical practices kept by churches which supposedly hold the Bible as sacred truth. These compromises are unjustifiable from a Biblical standpoint. One can only assume the church authorities involved – and the parishioners who condone the practices – are more concerned with the social aspect of their church than with holding to religious truth.

Everything Else

Unfortunately, that is not the end of the list. In the mid-1800's, a German man named Jakob Lorber was supposedly visited by an angel preaching another gospel, and modern *Christian mysticism* (a form of universalism) was born. In the early 1900's, the wife of a man named Herbert Armstrong had a spiritual revelation that one must keep the Ten Commandments in addition to accepting Christ in order to be saved, and the *Worldwide Church of God* was born. In the mid-1900's, a Korean man named Sun Myung Moon was supposedly visited by Jesus Christ himself in a vision and informed that the sacrifice of Jesus was only part of the price for salvation, and to be truly saved a person needed to join the new *Unification Church* that Moon was to start.

Then there are those cults you see on the news from time to time who have barricaded themselves in somewhere against a police standoff and decide to commit mass suicide in the name of their religious beliefs. These cults typically teach that some part of the Bible is true, but not other parts, and the leader is a man blessed with the ability to tell us which is which.

The list goes on and on. This is the kind of stuff that makes atheists feel intellectually superior to religious people. It is difficult to blame them in this respect. If an atheist never bothers to investigate religious truth from a logical perspective, and only goes by what he sees in his surrounding culture, his position would certainly seem reasonable on the surface. Religion looks pretty wacky at first glance, and much of it is.

We, however, took the time to investigate, and discovered the Bible to be logically irrefutable religious truth. We then took a look at some of the most popular Bible modifications and claims of further revelations, and found them to be wholly lacking in credibility. Modifications of the gospel message were revealed to be sorrowfully – and dangerously – illogical. We didn't get to all of them, but we didn't need to. We discovered a pattern, and have no reason to suspect a variation from that pattern were we to continue further. These examples only served to reinforce the Bible as truth, and to confirm its prophetic message of many false teachings coming after it.

The Bible tells us the work of Jesus on the cross is complete. He now draws out *a bride* for himself through his church, made up of those believers who have personally received and put their trust in him. When that process is complete, he will permanently join himself with his church and then physically return to the earth to set up his kingdom. Understanding this, one cannot logically conceive of a further revelation consistent with this knowledge – not before the process of drawing out a bride for Christ is complete, anyway. Such a revelation could only serve to supplant the truth and sabotage the work currently in progress. The result would be unfulfilled (or significantly altered) prophecy, which is a nullification of the prior truth. Truth by definition cannot be altered. This is obviously why the Bible warned of subsequent false teachings which would use the name of Christ.

It is not possible to "modify" the Bible in a way consistent with what it already teaches. The very act of modification changes the nature of something. We

132

have already proven the Bible as truth. To modify the truth is to render it inaccurate, which means it was not truth to begin with. We have already seen a variety of examples of this.

The Bible needs no further revelation, only sound exposition.

Conclusion

We have discovered religious truth, using nothing more than our intellect to analyze information which is widely available. By organizing our search in an efficient manner, the religious truth we sought was discovered in the first logical place we looked. This only further strengthens the already-conclusive evidence we found, because finding a convicting truth would become progressively harder the longer we were forced to search. This is due in part to the complications of additional logic problems which would be introduced by the notion of a creator who did not provide the religious truth in an easy-to-find manner. If our creator was not cooperative in making the truth available, it is unlikely to be discoverable at all. If our creator simply didn't care whether we had the truth or not, then even if we were able to discover it, it is unlikely to be beneficial. Only the existence of a loving and benevolent creator makes the discovery of important religious truth something we can reasonably hope to achieve – and in that case, it figures be available at or near the first natural place we think to look, as long as our search is conducted in a rational manner.

The Bible corroborates this line of reasoning as well. There are passages which state that *the heavens declare the glory of God and the firmament shows His handiwork,* and *the fool says in his heart, there is no God.* One particularly noteworthy verse about the evidence of God is:

Romans 1:20: *For his invisible attributes, namely, his eternal power and divine nature, have been clearly perceived, ever since the creation of the world, in the things that have been made. So they are without excuse. – ESV*

The above verse begins to ring familiar at this point, for it was the simple act of looking around and acknowledging that we exist which prompted us to start this project in the first place. Here, the Bible seems to be stating that non-belief in God is inexcusable, as the obvious fact we exist should be evidence enough. Albert Einstein seemed to agree, as he is quoted as saying *it is impossible for our universe not to have been created,* although his personal beliefs about God gravitated more towards a panentheistic viewpoint. (How highly intelligent men can miss the plainly logical truth of the Bible being true will be discussed in the last chapter.)

Revisiting our list of primary candidates at the beginning of this section, we can immediately dismiss any beliefs which conflict with the known truth. This is a simple, logical process of elimination. Conflicting beliefs cannot both be true. Consequently, any belief which conflicts with Biblical Christianity is now known to be false, and of course that includes all the rest of them. There is no need to go looking for truth after it has been found, so we have no compelling reason to explore the rest of the world's religions, other than perhaps pure academic curiosity. This book is not meant to be reference material, but a logical deduction process seeking truth. To that end, we will suspend with any such activities and instead pursue the more important matters implicated by the truth we have just discovered.

That being said, there is an interesting leftover from our list of primary candidates which deserves a brief discussion. When we found the Old Testament to be truth, we validated Judaism. When we found the New Testament to be a continuation of that truth, we invalidated Judaism, leaving it behind. It was God's true religion at one time, but God's own people failed miserably at it, so God had to come save us Himself. To revert to Judaism now is an exercise in futility, a case of too little too late, and is a rejection of God's solution for the salvation of man. We already tried that and it didn't work out, so God extended His grace to us in such a marvelous fashion that all we need to do is accept it. Refusing the grace and going back to try and practice the supplanted religion at this late date can be properly viewed as an ironic form of rebellion.

Judaism Revisited

In Israel today, a minority of the Jewish population still practices Judaism. A poll in 2009 revealed that over 60% of the Jewish population did not consider themselves to be religious. That figure includes roughly 25% of the Jewish population who adhere to Jewish religious traditions without holding a belief in the religion. The results of this poll indicate that most Jews in Israel today do not believe in God. It is an irony that resonates with much of their Biblical history, like something straight out of the book of II Kings.

A minority, however, does believe in the Hebrew Scriptures, and the individuals who make up that minority do practice Judaism to some degree or another. Many Jews living in other countries around the world do as well. Those who believe are said to be *orthodox*. It is a fascinating reality that practicing orthodox Jews have a religion with only half the truth. Logically, a half-truth cannot constitute truth. It is sad to picture them in their vain attempt to obey the more than 600 Jewish laws of the Old Testament, and look for their promised messiah 2,000 years after he came and dwelt among them. Fortunately, small minorities of Jews have had their eyes opened and accepted Christ. Jews who become Christians are known as *messianic Jews*.

The New Testament does shed some light on this mystery. The messiah came to his own people first, but was rejected. So, he went out to the rest of the world to draw out a bride for himself. In judgment of His people, the Bible tells us God has since blinded their eyes to the truth to some degree. Somehow, this is all part of God's plan.

However, God still considers the Jews to be His people. He is not done with them. He has a special relationship with Israel, and the end-time events in the book of Revelation use Israel as center stage. If there is any hope at all of salvation by works, my money is on orthodox Jews who love God. (Don't try this at home, however. The Bible tells us each of us will be held responsible for the knowledge we do have, and you now know the truth.)

The fact Israel was gathered *from the four corners of the earth* to become a nation again in 1948, after having been gone for nearly 1,900 years, is one of the most remarkable Bible prophecies ever to be fulfilled, and it has happened in our generation (or close to it). If nothing else convinces you of Bible truth, that fact should do the trick. No other group of people in the history of mankind has been so scattered and yet retained their ethnic identity. It is this event that now places us in the end times, very near the last days, on the Biblical timeline.

How Should We then Live?

There are important implications from the results of our investigation. Our well-being is at stake, both now and in the eternity beyond this life. Having discovered the truth, we are without excuse if we fail to do anything with it. The Bible tells us to *work out our own salvation with fear and trembling*. Fortunately, this is as easy as accepting a gift.

The New Testament reveals salvation as a gift from God. The apostle Paul said: *We are saved by grace alone, not by works, lest any man should boast*. A gift by definition is something you do not pay for yourself. You cannot earn a gift. The only way to get a gift is for somebody to give it to you, and then not refuse it. Jesus was sacrificed for our sin. His death opened the doors of heaven to anyone who accepts the gift of salvation.

However, we must accept it. We have only two choices, to accept the gift or reject it. The gift is Jesus himself. To accept the sacrifice, we need to receive Jesus. In so doing, we acknowledge that his sacrifice was necessary. Is this that hard to do? Is it really all that difficult to admit we are sinners? Do we really think we don't need to have our sins forgiven?

Perhaps we can acknowledge our sin, but still be reluctant to humble ourselves before God. This is understandable. After all, we are sinners. The Bible tells us pride is the worst sin of all, the truth of which is only too self-evident. Pride can keep us from accepting the gift of salvation.

Perhaps we are willing to both acknowledge our sin and humble ourselves before God, but do not want to receive Christ. That may have worked in Old Testament times, but it won't now, according to the New Testament. God has gone to tremendous lengths to make forgiveness readily available to us in the form of His Son. After the resurrection, Jesus said: *All power and authority have been transferred to me.* He paid the price for us with his own blood. We have nowhere to go now but to him, since he is the one who purchased our redemption. Christ is the provision God made for us.

Everyone must come down on one side or the other on the issue of Jesus Christ. Jesus himself said: *Those who are not for me are against me.* There is no neutrality with Jesus; neutrality is rejection of him. He claimed to be the Son of God. One of his apostles (Philip) asked Jesus to show them the father and Jesus replied: *If you have seen me, you have seen the father.* You cannot separate the Father from the Son now – that was done once in payment for our sin, and will never happen again. Jesus told us: *He who believes me believes He who sent me.* The question we all need to answer is the one Jesus asked the apostle Peter: *Who do you say that I am?*

It greatly behooves us to say that Jesus is our Lord. Let us turn from our sin now, receive Christ, ask for forgiveness, and joyfully become one of his followers. Jesus said: *My sheep know the sound of my voice, and respond when I call.* Do you know the sound of his voice? Would you like to? You can get rid of your sin – all of it – right this very moment, and become one of Jesus' sheep. All you need to do is open a communication with God and ask to receive the gift of Jesus. Jesus said: *Whoever comes to me I will in no wise cast out.* A Prayer to God can be initiated through voice or just thought, with your head bowed or raised, on your knees, sitting or standing, it doesn't matter. Just think a thought toward God right now, direct it to Him, ask to be forgiven of your sins and ask Christ to come into your heart and save you. It is that easy.

The most common reason quoted for being reluctant to receive Christ is not so much unbelief, but a feeling that one has sinned too much to be forgiven. Many of us can emphasize with that feeling. The good news it, that feeling is wrong – so wrong, in fact, it is almost insulting. Jesus died for the sins of the entire world, of all ages. His true suffering in becoming separated from the Father surpasses anything the human mind can conceive. Your sins are not so special that Jesus failed in paying for them. This was a work of God. God does not fail. Your sins have been paid for! God is inviting you to be freed from them. He paid a great price to free you from them. Say that prayer.

Just how forgiven are we when we come to Christ? The Bible tells us all our sins are removed *so far as the east is removed from the west,* and they *shall be neither mentioned nor remembered no more.* Isn't that glorious? Say that prayer!

If you did just say that prayer for the first time, I want to welcome you to the family of God. John's Gospel asserts that all who believe and accept Christ are *given the right to become the children of God.* Rest assured, your new family is thrilled to have you here. Nobody was any more deserving than anybody else, so we rejoice at our family enlarging by the mercy and grace of God.

Saying the sinner's prayer and receiving Christ is easier than living the Christian life, though. The world around us is wicked and full of unrepentant sinners. To make matters worse, there is a powerful enemy here who has made it his sole purpose is to derail and destroy all of us. The enemy doesn't need to focus all that much on unrepentant sinners. If you are a new Christian, however, you can expect to have some obstacles thrown your way. This is why Jesus said: *Pick up your cross and follow me.* Don't expect everything to go smoothly while living in this world, especially as a new believer. Do keep in mind, however, that *greater is He that is in you than he that is in the world.*

Jesus told the parable of the sower, as is recorded in three of the Gospels, to illustrate the dangers a new believer faces. Many who receive the good news don't

142

have it sink in, and the message of salvation is taken away as quickly as seeds which fall by the roadside are eaten by birds. Other seeds fall on rocky soil and sprout, but they have no depth of root, so the enemy has an easy time killing that newborn faith by simply tossing a few troubles at the person. Still other seeds take root and grow among thorns, the thorns being the cares of this world and the deceit of riches, which eventually choke out the new plant of faith. Finally, some seeds fall on good soil and grow into a thriving tree which ultimately produces fruit. If you are a new believer, you want to be the good soil that the seeds of salvation have fallen on.

This world is not our home. We are just passing through. Meanwhile, we sojourn in a hostile environment. Your faith can grow and flourish in this environment, if you take good care of it. If you don't, it will probably wither and die. Ignore your relationship with God, do nothing, don't attend a church or Bible study, never read your Bible, don't listen to Christian radio or watch Christian television, and your faith will probably wither and die as seeds that fell on rocky soil or among the thorn bushes. Don't let that happen.

Having your sins forgiven felt great, didn't it? Hold on to that feeling. Draw close to the Lord. God said: *Draw near to me and I will draw near to you.* Find a church you like. Listen to Bible studies on the internet and read Christian literature. Read the Bible (starting with the Gospels). Listen to Christian radio and/or watch Christian television. Grow in the Lord. Develop a sophisticated, child-like faith so you will be able to weather the storms of this life and remain close to God. There is no other pursuit which is truly satisfying. This one is.

Knowing what we know, we need to step back and reorganize our priorities in a rational manner. Jesus said: *Fear not those who can kill the body and do nothing more, but fear Him who can cast your soul into eternal hell.* I believe he was trying to help us get our priorities straight when he said that. Whatever we have going on in our life that is more important than God is a priority out of whack. We know God exists and the Bible is true, so we need to act accordingly. In that light, what else could possibly be so important? The Bible is God's own book, but more than that, it is a living, breathing entity which is sharper than any two-edged sword. Let us consult it regularly, and approach it with reverence.

Develop a prayer life. Pray regularly. It's easy. Once you start doing it, prayer becomes second nature. You can have a conversation with God at any time. The Bible tells us He wants to hear from us, early and often. Let's get Him more involved in our everyday life. Things can only improve.

You will find no better source of empowerment for your life than the combination of habitual prayer and Bible study. That's a promise.

Solving Deception and Unbelief

While we have solved the issues of existence and religion, we have yet to explore the mysteries of deception and unbelief. As mentioned several times in this text, many otherwise smart people hold obviously illogical religious beliefs, and some highly intelligent men refuse to acknowledge creation even after they have proved it to themselves. How can this be?

The Bible frequently speaks of the *heart* of man. This is not a reference to the organ in our chest which circulates our blood, nor does it pertain to intellect. Man's heart is something different than man's mind. The Bible tells us *every way of man is right in his own eyes, but the Lord weighs the heart* (or as another translation puts it, *the Lord weighs the spirit*). The heart of man is separate from the intelligence of man.

Emotions can be attributed to our heart. A markedly intelligent person is not necessarily someone who has their emotions under control. This is a mystery, but it does reveal an additional dimension to our being. A rational person becoming noticeably upset over an insignificant matter would seem to be an inconceivable event, but, as we all know, it is a common occurrence, one which causes many of us to smile knowingly as we recall our own such embarrassing moments. Everyone is guilty of it. We often kick ourselves in the behind for behavior we darn well know is illogical.

It is the heart of man God is primarily concerned with. Otherwise, only intellectuals would go to heaven. The fact both intelligent atheists and intelligent Christians exist, in addition to intelligent practitioners of every other major religion, attests to the existence of another dimension of man, other than our intellect. Our emotions are responsible for many important decisions we make, oftentimes in direct defiance to the instructions for our brains.

A perfect example is the quote from Dr. George Wald in the *Solving Existence* section of this text. A Nobel-prize winning professor of evolutionary science at Harvard University can confidently be categorized as an intelligent man. He admitted publicly that what he believes and teaches has proven to be impossible – yet he chooses to believe that which he knows to be false rather than acknowledge the only possible alternative, creation, because *he does not want to believe in God*. It doesn't matter if God stands in front of Him and says, "Here I am, believe in me," (and from Dr. Wald's perspective, God has virtually done just that). His position is entirely irrational and he admits it to be so, yet his intelligence cannot be denied. One must attribute his decision as being an emotional one, a defiance of his very intellect, a reflection of his heart.

146

That intelligent men can allow their emotions to overrule their intellect is supporting evidence of what the Bible says about men's hearts. It is also convincing testimony of the existence of man's eternal spirit. The heart of man is part of his eternal nature. The brain is part of the physical body and rots away with the corpse after death. This is why God is concerned with our heart more than our mind. The heart is responsible for emotions such as love, compassion, and rebellion. To align one's heart with God is to connect with the eternal source of nourishment; to turn one's heart away from God is to sever oneself from that source.

The Bible tells us in many passages that man's heart is inherently wicked. We are bad by nature. God is good by nature, however, and capable of cleansing our heart. God did not intend for us to be wicked, but he did intend for us to possess free will. He wanted real children who freely choose to love Him, not robots or dolls with pull strings who say *I love you*, and giving us free will was the only way to accomplish that. This necessitated that rebellion was a possible choice for us to make. With free will being an indispensable part of our makeup, it was inevitable that bad decisions would be made. The very first man and woman exercised their free will in making a bad decision to disobey God, and the result is the fallen world we now live in.

Man isn't the only rebel among God's creatures. God also created angels with free will, and the same result – rebellion – appears to have been just as inevitable.

The Old Testament chapters of Isaiah 14 and Ezekiel 28 tell us about Satan's fall from grace. He was a beautiful cherub angel, and perhaps the most powerful of all God's creations. He became prideful and attempted to exalt himself above God, however, and was cast down as a result. Other Bible passages tell us he was successful in recruiting one-third of the angels of heaven to join up and follow him in his rebellion before they all were cast out of heaven. Now they all reside here on earth among us. Satan is their leader. They are resolved to destroy us, because humans are an object of God's love and are so easily corruptible.

God never intended for bad things to happen or for evil to exist, but it was an unavoidable consequence of free will. All the terrible things we see in the world – sickness, starvation, persecution, murder, war – are all the result of God's creatures rebelling against him. God didn't bring any of that stuff into manifestation on earth; we did. Ultimately, it all became necessary in order for God to raise children who freely choose to love him. Those who freely choose to rebel have rendered the environment hostile for all of us. Ironically, it is those who are still in rebellion who typically complain against God and tend to blame Him for all the evil which they themselves brought about.

Non-belief can, therefore, properly be thought of as rebellion. Dr. Wald's statement sheds further light on this situation. Logically, in light of what we now know, someone who claims to be an atheist must either be a person who has not thought the situation through, or one who is simply displaying their rebellion. A rational person cannot cling to the theory of spontaneous generation of life followed by evolution as an explanation of our existence, because it has been scientifically and mathematically disproven. One can only cling to such a belief as a public showing of their rebellion against God, assuming they have even bothered to research it. Most non-believers will not bother to research the theory they claim to believe in, because they do not care if it is disproven. It is just something tangible upon which to hang their rebellion.

The end for the rebels is not a good one. It is an interesting observation that many do not care, and willingly trade away eternity in order to have their short period of rebellion. When Jesus was casting unclean spirits out of people in the Gospels, he would often confront the demons, and they recognized him. Some are recorded as begging Jesus not to send them to their eternal place of punishment *before their time.* They know where they are going, but would rather have their short time of rebellion now than repent and have an eternity of paradise. Many people are the same way.

Deception is a more complicated matter than unbelief. Our enemy has established many false religions as a way of trapping people into rejecting the gospel. No doubt, many who cling to some of these religions do it as a personal form of rebellion. One who knows the gospel message, but rejects it in favor

149

of a liberal theology of some type, may simply be performing their own personal brand of rebellion against God. This would seem to be the most likely explanation for intelligent people being found practicing clearly illogical religions, and in essence is no different than the practice of atheism. God knows our hearts.

Others may genuinely have been deceived by the false teachings, or were perhaps drawn in purely by an emotional attraction, and it is those whom we must attempt to reach with the message of the gospel somehow. (Feel free to give your copy of this book to any you might know.) God has placed His evangelists in all the places He needs them. You can do your part by just being willing, in whatever capacity God calls you, whether it is through witnessing to a coworker by the testimony of your own life, or through financial support of missionaries whose cause touches your heart. If you are willing to be a cog on a wheel in God's vast machinery someplace, He will find a place to put you to use. Keep in mind nobody is called to serve in a capacity which is unattractive to them.

The Bible tells us God is just, and no one will go to hell without being given the chance to accept or reject the gospel. How He accomplishes that is His business, but we can rest assured there will be no injustice with God. In fact, the Bible tells us that those of us who place our trust in Christ will all agree with God's ultimate judgment, and praise him joyfully for it. We serve a fair and righteous God.

About the Author

Now comes the part where I confess my lack of credentials. I am not a pastor or minister, and have never been ordained by any recognized body. I have never attended seminary or a brick-and-mortar Bible college. I do not have a college degree of any kind. The only Bible studies I have conducted have been quite small ones in my own home.

I am just a regular guy who has a passion for Bible study, and who has spent a considerable number of weekly hours dedicated to it over the last ten years. I am still on the potter's wheel being formed, into exactly what only God knows. If you learned new things about the Bible from this book, I am pleased. I encourage you to pursue your own spiritual development through the fervent study of God's Word. Maybe someday I will read one of your books. If you did not learn anything new about the Bible, I hope that the manner in which I presented this study opened new insights and provoked a thought process which will ultimately be profitable for you.

I believe Christians today place too much emphasis on doctrinal divisions between denominational interpretations of scripture, and not enough time loving our Christian brothers and sisters. Division within the body of Christ saddens me. We should be more burdened for the lost than we are concerned about our dogmatic viewpoints on eschatological timelines and sacramental doctrines. It is for this reason that I will not refer you to the popular (and anonymously-written) spiritual blog which I have been writing for years, as it is doctrinally slanted - and I wish for your opinion of me to be formed from the work I have presented in this volume.

I am a happily married man in my late forties. My wife and I are not wealthy, but we are tremendously blessed. I have found myself forced into too many career changes in my working life, but God always comes through for me, as He will you. Even during the bad times, I have been able to remain faithful in all areas of my Christian walk. Money has not been a problem for us; we always seem to have enough, and God always comes through with a new exciting income source for me. My wife and I enjoy travel, especially in Europe - where we go every couple of years for a nice vacation of some sort.

This world is not our home. I wish you tremendous blessings in your pilgrimage here. May the Lord make you happy, healthy, and prosperous today, tomorrow, and forever.

Paul Kasch

Made in the USA
Middletown, DE
10 January 2017